D0506378

Show Me The Way

Show Me The Way

PATHWAYS THROUGH MY LIFE

Wendy Craig

Hodder & Stoughton
LONDON SYDNEY AUCKLAND

British Library Cataloguing in Publication Data
A record for this book is available from the British Library

ISBN 0 340 863943

Typeset in Galliard by Avon DataSet Ltd,
Bidford on Avon, Warwickshire

Printed and bound in Great Britain by
Clays Ltd, St Ives plc

The paper used in this book is a natural recyclable product
made from wood grown in sustainable forests. The hard
coverboard is recycled.

Hodder & Stoughton
A Division of Hodder Headline Ltd
338 Euston Road
London NW1 3BH
www.madaboutbooks.com

This book is dedicated to my family and friends
with gratitude for their love and understanding

Acknowledgements

My sincere thanks must go to Chris for his help in compiling and making sense of all the thoughts and information I threw in his direction. He's a good catcher! Chris would like to thank his family, Charlie Casey, Katherine Mansi and Dave Berry for their personal support and encouragement. We would both like to thank Sally Goring at 'Christians in Entertainment', who is always ready to listen and pray; and my publisher Judith Longman at Hodder and Stoughton for her faith in, and patience with, this book.

While every effort has been made to contact the copyright holders of material used in this book, this has not always been successful. Full acknowledgment will gladly be made in future editions.

Unless otherwise indicated, Scripture quotations are taken from: *Good News Bible: Today's English Version with Deuterocanonicals/ Apocrypha*, (edited by Robert G. Bratcher) © 1979 American Bible Society. Used by permission.

Other versions used are:
AV – Authorised Version
NIV – New International Version. Copyright © 1973, 1978, 1984 by International Bible Society. Used by permission.
The Message, copyright © by Eugene H. Peterson 1993, 1994, 1995, NavPress Publishing Group. Used by permission.

We also gratefully acknowledge the following:

John Betjeman, 'Diary of a church mouse' in *Collected Poems* © 2003 John Murray. Used by permission.

Leslie F. Brandt, 'Psalm 51' and 'Psalm 85', *Psalms Now* (3rd edition) © 2004 Concordia Publishing. Used by permission.

Foreword

by Chris Gidney

Wendy Craig is one of this country's best-loved actresses, and with such a long and distinguished career in television, theatre and film it's easy to see why. Remembering such television classics as *Not in Front of the Children*, *And Mother Makes Three*, as well as the much acclaimed *Nanny* and *Butterflies*, Wendy Craig is still everybody's favourite mum. These hilarious series are being rerun on television for a new generation to enjoy, while Wendy treats us to her current role as the matriarchal matron in *The Royal*, now in its fifth series for ITV. Wendy's stage appearances stretch from the Royal Shakespeare Company to London's West End and back again.

Alongside her commercial success, I have seen over many years of friendship how Wendy's professional and personal life is built on a Christian faith that Wendy describes as 'a never-ending resource for my life today'.

I know she is tremendously thankful to have enjoyed such a long career in a profession that is known for being so transient. Helping an audience to laugh, cry and think about different aspects of life is a God-given gift that she enjoys using very much. Not that she would say so herself. Wendy is a very modest person, often struggling with feelings of personal worth, which is what makes a volume like this so real. Her honesty about her feelings and failures means that this is a book that everybody can relate to.

Having been convinced of the existence of God at a tender age, Wendy's faith was eventually squeezed out by the demands of acting and fame. Somehow, amid busy family life and success, God was no longer relevant.

Some years later something changed inside her and the need to take another look at her spiritual foundations became vitally important. For a while, Wendy experienced a deep emptiness inside, and an acute lack of direction. Even though she tried to brush away these feelings with excuses about a mid-life crisis, they just wouldn't leave her. These feelings gnawed away and made her feel anxious and depressed, but she felt unable to do anything about them. She felt trapped and helpless.

It was a personal tragedy that finally brought these feelings to a head, and one day she found herself sitting alone at the back of her local church. Wendy started to beg God to help her, and as she did so, all the sadness, misery and guilt she had carried for so long began to fall away.

In the following weeks, Wendy came to understand that God still cared about her in spite of the fact that she had turned her back on Him in the past. Seeing that forgiveness was there for the asking, she grabbed at it. Along the way, she was richly supported by Christian friends who rallied around her and was also much encouraged by books, Bible readings, audio cassettes, personal thoughts, experiences and prayers. Wendy learned that God didn't want to interfere or control her life, but just desired to be a heavenly Father who wanted his child back. She became aware that he alone could bring her peace and guidance in all the bewildering pathways of life, through which she walks.

For some reason Wendy didn't get involved in any of the other forms of 'spiritual support', such as lucky charms or fortune stones. Even though there is plenty of superstition in the theatre world, Wendy kept her childhood faith in its most basic form and just sent up a simple prayer. 'I'm glad that I did,' she says, 'Because when my life started to crumble from inside, I knew where to turn for help.'

Show me the Way was one of the songs that Wendy found herself writing during a time of spiritual reflection. It was a particularly difficult period of her life and the lyrics of the song that came to her are a clear and concise request for guidance, reassurance, healing and love – essentials that Wendy says she needs on a daily basis.

This book is Wendy's way of sharing some of the things that have not only carried her through the bumpy pathway of life, but brought her a living, joyful and vibrant reassurance in an unsteady and often confusing world.

Introduction

Show Me The Way is my personal collection of inspirational and sometimes humorous writing that has encouraged my journey and is entwined around my memories and experiences. Some of the pieces I have selected are old favourites, some brand new. Many of the old hymns I have chosen here are very familiar, but take a closer look at the words because I have found that reading them through rather than singing them offers a different insight.

All the pieces I have chosen have played a part in reminding me of the important things in life that are helping me through. I make no apology for offering most of this volume with a strong spiritual foundation. I have found that while it is easy to concentrate on one's mind and body, all too often it's our spirit that we neglect.

So, I hope that this small anthology will help cheer your spirit also as you walk along life's pathways, and discover just how much God cares about you every step of the way.

'Show me the Way'

This song came to me one day while walking in the countryside with my dog. I was asking God for his guidance, and as I was praying I began to sing. The tune and the words came to me out of the blue, and when I got home I could still remember them. I sang them on to a cassette, and my son Ross transcribed them and wrote a simple arrangement for me.

Years later I spoke the words on BBC's *Songs of Praise* accompanied by my son Alaster on the oboe, and I was overwhelmed at the response from viewers who felt the lyrics touched their own thoughts and feelings. It is a simple request to God to show me the way:

> When I'm confused, Lord, show me the way
> Show me, show me, the way
> Baffled and bruised, Lord, show me the way
> Show me, show me, show me the way
>
> Still my heart and clear my mind
> Prepare my soul to hear
> Your still, small voice
> Your word of truth
> Peace be still your Lord is here.
> Always so close to show you the way
> Show you, show you, show you the way

When I'm afraid, Lord
Show me the way
Show me, show me, show me the way
Weak and dismayed, Lord
Show me the way
Show me, show me, show me the way

Lift my spirit with your love
Bring courage, calm and peace
You who bore all for my sake
So I could walk from fear released
With you beside me
Showing the way
Showing, showing, showing the way

Wendy Craig

Hang on to your dreams

Our earliest experiences are often the ones that have the greatest impact on the rest of our lives. Looking back over my childhood, and also reflecting on the things that my own children and grandchildren did, provides me with a wonderful resource of laughter and happy memories.

My life as an actor started almost as soon as I was aware that such a thing existed. I was taken to my first pantomime at the age of three. It immediately awoke in me a love of the theatre. A bubble of excitement became an overwhelming desire to jump up on to that stage and join the dancers and comics in their glittering costumes under the lights. I had to be restrained, but that night when I was in my pyjamas I re-enacted the whole story for my parents, playing all the parts – and even imagining I could perform the antics of the contortionist!

My bewildered mum and dad thought that I was over-excited and would never be able to sleep. I slept, however, wonderfully well, with perhaps a few magical dreams of holding the attention of an audience as I sang and pirouetted across the stage in a frilly frock. Little did I know that one day that dream was to become a reality.

Some would say that dreams are like poetry as they speak in the same mother tongue of metaphor and use strong visual imagery. In the Bible, God used dreams to talk to those he loved, and I'm sure he sometimes does the same today. Here's a short dream poem that makes me feel free from life's cares:

I dream in the clouds
so soft, so calm
I'm free to float to wherever
and I dream in the clouds

I cast away all thoughts, earthly chained
and dream of heavenly salvation
I caress the air that I can not see
yet I know surrounds me
and with a gentle longing
I dream in the clouds

Author unknown

Open arms

It was my granny who first taught me about Jesus. She had been the headmistress of the village school, but now was retired and she and Grandad had come to live with my parents in the little three-bedroomed house at Sacriston, County Durham. I was very young, maybe four or five, and I loved her because she was calm and gentle and made a big fuss of my brother and me.

My mother had converted the back bedroom into a sort of bed-sitter, and Granny, who sadly became blind as a result of cataracts, used to sit in an armchair with a rug over her knees knitting squares to make blankets for the soldiers. The Second World War was imminent and she was determined to do her bit. I loved to climb on to her knee and brush her silver hair while she spoke to me about her friend Jesus. She retold the parables and Bible stories that first awoke in me an awareness of the Christian faith and a desire to know Jesus as personally as she did. In her trembly voice she sang hymns to me, hymns full of certainty and joy. I never wanted her to stop, and had to be prised away by my mother in case I made Granny too tired.

Looking back, Granny reminds me of how Jesus always accepted the little ones and even rebuked his disciples when they suggested the master was too busy to see them. Granny was never too busy to spend time with me either, and this was one of my favourites that I begged she sing over and over to me:

Jesus, Friend of little children,
be a friend to me;
take my hand, and ever keep me
close to thee.

Teach me how to grow in goodness,
daily as I grow;
thou hast been a child, and surely
thou dost know.

Never leave me, nor forsake me;
ever be my friend;
for I need thee, from life's dawning
to its end.

Walter J. Mathams

One prayer covers all

My brother Allistair and I shared a room when we were small. He was four years older than me. We would lie awake at night talking and laughing before we dropped off to sleep. He told me what he'd done at school that day and the things he'd learnt. He taught me how to sing 'Shenandore' and 'What Shall We Do with the Drunken Sailor?'

He also taught me to recite the 23rd Psalm and the Lord's Prayer. I repeated them parrot fashion, having little concept of their meaning. Only later did they become clear to me. My dear brother died suddenly at the age of 68. I shall always be grateful to him for teaching me those words. They are a precious legacy.

I was interested to read that the Convent of Pater Noster was built over the site where Jesus first taught his disciples the Lord's Prayer. The walls are decorated with 140 ceramic tiles, each one inscribed with the Lord's Prayer in a different language. The Convent has spent the last ten years attempting to translate these words into as many languages and dialects as possible. To date, they have 1,316 versions, which proves it must be the most universal prayer for all of humanity.

Many have reproduced their own versions of the Lord's Prayer. I even discovered that in the 1960s the American group, the Beach Boys, recorded their own version in a song! Here's one that I particularly enjoy reading from a German translation reportedly used by Rudolf Steiner in his daily spiritual practice in 1924–5:

Father, you who were, are, and will be
in our inmost being
May your name be glorified
and praised in us

May your kingdom grow
in our deeds and in our moral lives
May we perform your will
as you, Father, lay it down
in our inmost being

You give us spiritual nourishment,
the bread of life
superabundantly
in all the changing conditions
of our lives

Let our mercy toward others
make up for the sins done to our being
Let not the tempter
work in us beyond the capacity of our strength

For no temptation can live
in your being, Father,
and the tempter is only appearance
and delusion,
from which you lead us, Father
by the light of knowledge

May your power and glory
work in us through all eons and eons of time.
Amen

Coloured glass

My first experience of church was not a very religious one. I remember it was on my birthday, and I must have been about four. Mum and Dad had bought me a kilt and a little Harris tweed jacket. I stood at home in the Lindsay tartan that was my mother's clan and felt very proud.

'She looks lovely,' I heard my mother say to George, my dad. 'Take her down to the church this morning.' The idea was to show me off to the village and going to church was the best way to do it.

We walked hand in hand down to Sacriston village church and I soon found myself sitting on the hard wooden pew. I copied everyone as they stood up or sat down, knelt or sang hymns, having absolutely no idea what was going on. They didn't have family services in those days; children were expected to sit through Matins without a squeak.

I grew restless during the sermon, so Daddy leant across to me and whispered, 'Look at those lovely coloured stained glass windows, Wendy.' I spent the rest of the service gazing up at the beautiful sight and trying to recognise some of the more familiar Bible characters from the things my granny had taught me. I thought I could see Jesus, his disciples, and a few other things like flowers and angels. What I didn't recognise I soon made into make-believe stories. It was a wonderful way to spend my first visit to church and I became aware of a God who was vivid and colourful.

Here, the evangelist, Dan Kimball, explains how he had a similar experience much later in his life:

As I sat there looking at the ten or so stained glass panels of people throughout church history, I began wondering what would my stained glass image be? Would it show someone who was always rushing around and flustered? Would it show someone who was always tired? What symbols would be shown to represent me and my heart? I sat for a long time and prayed, finally able to focus my thoughts as I did some self-reflection. As I quieted my soul looking at the beauty of the stained glass images, my mind went to some passages in Ephesians. I reflected on the fact that we are God's 'workmanship' created in Christ in advance for good works he prepared for us to do (Ephesians 2:10). The word 'workmanship' comes from the very word we get 'poem' from. I sat and thought how we are all poems, and pieces of art that God created like the stained glass. Each piece of art created for a purpose. I reflected how in Ephesians 3:10 that we, the church, are even on display before the angelic realm. God's pieces of art, his stained glass poetry, each of us a panel on display to the heavenlies as we fulfil the purpose he created us in advance to do. I looked closer at the stained glass panels, and realised the pieces in themselves were not what was beautiful. In fact, the individual glass pieces on their own are not too pretty at all. But, like the sin-'stained' human beings we are, God assembles broken pieces like us into beautiful images – his workmanship – used for his glory. And what makes the stained glass beautiful is not the glass itself either, but the sunlight shining through them. Like us, without Jesus shining through us, we are only sin-stained and not beautiful, but with Jesus, God uses us, his artwork, for a purpose and to be on display to the angelic realm.

How times have changed

When I was five I was sent to Durham High School for Girls for the first year. I used to travel by bus each day with my cousin, Margaret. Sacriston was a mining village, and when I could read I was surprised as I slowly deciphered a sign in the bus saying 'Hawking and Spitting Prohibited!' Many of the miners suffered with respiratory diseases, and so spitting on the streets and in public transport was quite commonplace. How times have changed. Thankfully, in a much more health-conscious age, workers are largely protected from such industrial illnesses.

However, not everything in our society has changed for the better, and one of the most reassuring truths in our transient world is that God never changes. His love and goodness are as reliable today as they ever were. God isn't swayed by all the whims and fancies of our world. He is the same yesterday, today and for ever. What a comfort!

GOD IS UNCHANGING

Let nothing disturb you, nothing alarm you:
While all things fade away
God is unchanging.
Be patient
And you will gain everything:
For with God in your heart

Nothing is lacking,
God meets your every need.

St Teresa of Avila
(modern version by Henry Wadsworth Longfellow)

The sanctuary knocker

Durham Cathedral dominates the whole town from its point on the hill. The Great North Door still has its sanctuary knocker, and I love to touch it whenever I return. Fugitives, running away from the law, would race to the cathedral and grab hold of the knocker. Once inside the sanctuary, they were safe for thirty-seven days.

Forty years after leaving Durham High School, as I viewed the cathedral while waiting for the film crew to arrive for a BBC *Songs of Praise*, it still held its atmosphere of welcoming safety. Sitting alone, I was reminded of all the songs I sang in that ancient building. Songs about turning to God in the storms of life, and finding safety and sanctuary in him. As a schoolgirl, little did I know just how relevant the need to find sanctuary would be for me in later life.

You need to be healthy to manage Durham Cathedral's impressive tower. When I was young, its 325 steps didn't bother me too much, but now I don't recommend it to those whose hearts are not as strong as they might be! The steps are very steep and move relentlessly upwards. Sometimes life seems to be like that. We climb and climb, and still feel that we are getting absolutely nowhere. When I reached the top of the Durham Tower it afforded the most spectacular view, and so it was worth all the effort in the end. With God's help we shall be overcomers. So when you are feeling overwhelmed by the exhaustion of life, don't look down, or give up, keep looking up and keep on going!

I will lift up mine eyes unto the hills, from whence
 cometh my help.
My help cometh from the Lord, which made heaven and
 earth.
He will not suffer thy foot to be moved: he that keepeth
 thee will not slumber.
Behold, he that keepeth Israel shall neither slumber nor
 sleep.
The Lord is thy keeper: the Lord is thy shade upon thy
 right hand.
The sun shall not smite thee by day, nor the moon by
 night.
The Lord shall preserve thee from all evil: he shall
 preserve thy soul.
The Lord shall preserve thy going out and thy coming
 in from this time forth, and even for evermore.

Psalm 121, AV

Story time

My first teacher at Durham High School was Miss Morgan. She was bonny and buxom with black curls and plump rosy cheeks. She used to read aloud to us while we sat cross-legged on the floor around her, trying to get as close to her as possible. I still remember with great affection her lively portrayal of Toad, Ratty, etc. in *The Wind in the Willows*. The book was so beautiful, and parts of it had an almost spiritual quality that appealed to me greatly.

When I played 'Nanny' in the BBC series of the same name, I read *The Wind in the Willows* to the old Duke as he was dying. I thought it was a sensitive touch from the writers Charlotte Bingham and Terence Brady to include it in such a tender scene.

Breathless and transfixed the Mole stopped rowing as the liquid run of that glad piping broke on him like a wave, caught him up, and possessed him utterly. He saw the tears on his comrade's cheeks, and bowed his head and understood. For a space they hung there, brushed by the purple loosestrife that fringed the bank; then the clear imperious summons that marched hand-in-hand with the intoxicating melody imposed its will on Mole, and mechanically he bent to his oars again. And the light grew steadily stronger, but no birds sang as they were wont to do at the approach of dawn; and but for the heavenly music all was marvellously still.

On either side of them, as they glided onwards, the rich meadow grass seemed that morning of a freshness and a greenness unsurpassable. Never had they noticed the roses so vivid, the willow-herb so riotous, the meadow-sweet so odorous and pervading. The murmur of the approaching weir began to hold the air, and they felt a consciousness that they were nearing the end, whatever it might be, that surely awaited their expedition.

A wide half-circle of foam and glinting lights and shining shoulders of green water, the great weir closed the backwater from bank to bank troubled all the quiet surface with twirling eddies and floating foam-streaks, and deadening all other sounds with its solemn and soothing rumble. In midmost of the stream, embraced in the weir's shimmering arm spread, a small island lay anchored, fringed close with willow and silver birch and alder. Reserved, shy, but full of significance, it hid whatever it might hold behind a veil, keeping it till the hour should come, and, with the hour, those who were called and chosen.

Slowly, but with no doubt or hesitation whatever, and in something of a solemn expectancy, the two animals passed through the broken, tumultuous water and moored their boat at the flowery margin of the island. In silence they landed, and pushed through the blossom and scented herbage and undergrowth that led up to the level ground, till they stood on a little lawn of a marvellous green, set round with Nature's own orchard-trees – crab apple, wild cherry, and sloe.

'This is the place of my song-dream, the place the music played to me,' whispered the Rat, as if in a trance. 'Here in this holy place, here if anywhere, surely we shall find Him!'

Kenneth Graham

Unreserved confidence

The school hall at Durham was a long wooden hut adjacent to the main house. It served as a gymnasium, theatre and chapel. It was here that I did my first play in front of an audience of doting parents and relatives. It was called *The Little Red Hen* and guess who played the leading fowl?

Even at the age of five, I was developing signs of becoming a thespian. I was so confident in my part, and so much in charge of things, I fluttered on to the stage in my little hen costume, and when any of the others dried up, I was in there like a shot with their line too. Unfortunately, my helpfulness just caused more problems by throwing the others out of sequence. In the end they all gave up and I did the entire play myself. The parents of the other children were furious. 'That precocious child!' they muttered. I was oblivious to all this and just noticed my parents' faces glowing with pride at the completion of the performance.

My confidence for life at that time came from my parents who instilled it into me with love. I have them and my teachers to be thankful to, and it's a reminder for all of us that when we become parents and grandparents ourselves, how we can so easily destroy or build up a child.

IF A CHILD . . .

If a child lives with criticism,
she learns to condemn.
If a child lives with hostility,
she learns to fight.
If a child lives with ridicule,
she learns to be shy.
If a child lives with shame,
she learns to feel guilty.
If a child lives with tolerance,
she learns to be patient.
If a child lives with encouragement,
she learns confidence.
If a child lives with praise,
she learns to appreciate.
If a child lives with fairness,
she learns justice.
If a child lives with security,
she learns to have faith.
If a child lives with approval,
she learns to like herself.
If a child lives with acceptance and friendship,
She learns to find love in the world.

Author unknown

Laughter in church

There's nothing I love more than a good laugh, but I'm a terrible giggler, and always have been. I do my best to control this when I'm working because laughing on stage is bad manners, and holding up shooting with helpless laughter can be really irritating for the crew. Even as a child I was prone to the giggles and it caused me problems from time to time.

Every morning the whole school gathered for prayers. It was a traditional Church of England school and the short service was taken very seriously and was carefully prepared by the staff.

I was mortified one day when I was sent out of this assembly because of a fit of the giggles. I don't know what caused it. All I know is that I was helpless and almost crying with laughter. I still remember how appalled I felt as I stood outside the door red-faced with shame.

Although my laughter was inappropriate at the time, I do think we should have more laughter in church. Surely being a Christian is something to be joyful about?

This poem by John Betjeman highlights his delicious sense of irony and humour:

DIARY OF A CHURCH MOUSE

Here among the long discarded cassocks,
Damp stools, and half-split open hassocks,
Here where the vicar never looks
I nibble through old service books.
Lean and alone I spend my days
Behind this Church of England baize.
I share my dark forgotten room
With two oil-lamps and half a broom.
The cleaner never bothers me,
So here I eat my frugal tea.
My bread is sawdust mixed with straw;
My jam is polish for the floor.
Christmas and Easter may be feasts
For congregations and for priests,
And so may Whitsun. All the same,
They do not fill my meagre frame.
For me the only feast at all
Is Autumn's Harvest Festival,
When I can satisfy my want
With ears of corn around the font.
I climb the eagle's brazen head
To burrow through a loaf of bread.
I scramble up the pulpit stair
And gnaw the marrows hanging there
It is enjoyable to taste
These items ere they go to waste,
But how annoying when one finds
That other mice with pagan minds
Come into church my food to share
Who have no proper business there.
Two field mice who have no desire

To be baptized, invade the choir.
A large and most unfriendly rat
Comes in to see what we are at.
He says he thinks there is no God
And yet he comes . . . it's rather odd.
This year he stole a sheaf of wheat
(It screened our special preacher's seat),
And prosperous mice from fields away
Come in to hear the organ play,
And under cover of its notes
Ate through the altar's sheaf of oats.
A Low Church mouse, who thinks that I
Am too papistical, and High,
Yet somehow doesn't think it wrong
To munch through Harvest Evensong,
While I, who starve the whole year through,
Must share my food with rodents who
Except at this time of the year
Not once inside the church appear.
Within the human world I know
Such goings-on could not be so,
For human beings only do
What their religion tells them to.
They read the Bible every day
And always, night and morning, pray,
And just like me, the good church mouse,
Worship each week in God's own house,
But all the same it's strange to me
How very full the church can be
With people I don't see at all
Except at Harvest Festival.

John Betjeman

God's house

Durham High School for Girls was an old house set in a large garden on the bank of the River Wear. It was within the sound of the cathedral bells and on special occasions we would celebrate in that glorious building. As we entered one by one, the overwhelming feeling for me was one of awe and history. The cathedral has stood as a place of prayer and pilgrimage for over nine hundred years. With its astounding round stained glass window and tomb of Bede, the first English historian, it is one of the most beautiful buildings in England. No wonder, then, that Bill Bryson called Durham 'the best cathedral on planet earth'.

Most cathedrals have rather elegant columns supporting them, but Durham has huge, fat columns that are massively impressive. The first time I went into that building a shaft of sunlight was shining straight through the great wheel window and I thought, 'This must be where God lives. This must be his house.'

As our High School was closely affiliated with Durham Cathedral, we would often celebrate special school events there – such as feast days or speech days. We would make our way through Durham town centre and over the bridge to the cathedral in a long green crocodile. I was a dreamy child and used to imagine that I was a pilgrim on my way to worship at the sacred edifice. We had read John Bunyan's *Pilgrim's Progress*, and sometimes I pretended that I was on the pathway of the Celestial Country as we climbed the steep hill where we could see the splendour of the cathedral sitting right at the top.

John Bunyan wrote his famous book during his twelve-year

prison sentence for refusing to conform to the official State Church. Some of the original text from the *Pilgrim's Progress* was later turned into one of my favourite hymns:

He who would valiant be 'gainst all disaster,
Let him in constancy follow the Master.
There's no discouragement shall make him once relent
His first avowed intent to be a pilgrim.

Who so beset him round with dismal stories
Do but themselves confound – his strength the more is.
No foes shall stay his might; though he with giants fight,
He will make good his right to be a pilgrim.

Since, Lord, Thou dost defend us with Thy Spirit,
We know we at the end, shall life inherit.
Then fancies flee away! I'll fear not what men say,
I'll labour night and day to be a pilgrim.

'He who would valiant be', *John Bunyan
as modified in 1906 by Percy Dearmer*

Say it out loud

I just loved singing hymns and I still do. Our hymnbook was called *Songs of Praise* and because we had good music teachers who were passionate about what they played, the accompaniment was always superb. The voices and the instruments fired up a great enthusiasm in me to the point where one day during choir practice the teacher said, 'Wendy Craig. Please stop singing so loudly, you are spoiling it for the others!'

I was beside myself with embarrassment. I was just having a wonderful time, but at least I learnt that my voice was loud, and this information came in very handy in the years to come. However, it made me feel shy about singing and it wasn't until I did my first pantomime that I was persuaded to sing live by the lovely comedy actor Jack Douglas.

One of the hymns that would make me want to stand on my tiptoes with excitement was this one. It still does! I love to think that wherever people are waking up around the world, they carry worship around the clock. It's a constant flow of prayer and praise:

> Hills of the North, rejoice;
> River and mountain spring,
> Hark to the advent voice;
> Valley and lowland, sing;
> Though absent long, your Lord is nigh;
> He judgment brings and victory.

Isles of the southern seas,
Deep in your coral caves
Pent be each warring breeze,
Lulled be your restless waves:
He comes to reign with boundless sway,
And makes your wastes His great highway.

Lands of the East, awake,
Soon shall your sons be free;
The sleep of ages break,
And rise to liberty.
On your far hills, long cold and grey,
Has dawned the everlasting day.

Shores of the utmost West,
Ye that have waited long,
Unvisited, unblest,
Break forth to swelling song;
High raise the note, that Jesus died,
Yet lives and reigns, the Crucified.

Shout, while ye journey home;
Songs be in every mouth;
Lo, from the North we come,
From East, and West, and South.
City of God, the bond are free,
We come to live and reign in thee!

Charles E. Oakley

Protection for life

St Patrick's Breastplate was the school hymn at Durham High School. We sang it on every special occasion at school and always on the last day of term. It still brings a lump to my throat when I think of the sad parting from friends who were leaving for one reason or another. It was comforting to know that the Lord would be watching over them as they left the seclusion of our Christian school to go into the outside world:

> I bind unto myself today
> The strong Name of the Trinity,
> By invocation of the same
> The Three in One, and One in Three.
>
> I bind unto myself today
> The virtues of the star lit heaven,
> The glorious sun's life giving ray,
> The whiteness of the moon at even,
> The flashing of the lightning free,
> The whirling wind's tempestuous shocks,
> The stable earth, the deep salt sea
> Around the old eternal rocks.
>
> I bind unto myself today
> The power of God to hold and lead,
> His eye to watch, His might to stay,
> His ear to hearken to my need.
> The wisdom of my God to teach,
> His hand to guide, His shield to ward;

The word of God to give me speech,
His heavenly host to be my guard.

Christ be with me, Christ within me,
Christ behind me, Christ before me,
Christ beside me, Christ to win me,
Christ to comfort and restore me.
Christ beneath me, Christ above me,
Christ in quiet, Christ in danger,
Christ in hearts of all that love me,
Christ in mouth of friend and stranger.

I bind unto myself the Name,
The strong Name of the Trinity,
By invocation of the same,
The Three in One and One in Three.
By Whom all nature hath creation,
Eternal Father, Spirit, Word:
Praise to the Lord of my salvation,
Salvation is of Christ the Lord.

Cecil F. Alexander

Consistency works

In my childhood home, Monday was washing day. Tuesday was ironing day. Wednesday was baking day. Thursday was mending day, and Friday was getting-ready-for-the-weekend day in preparation for visitors.

There is something wonderful about this sort of tradition that brings an order to life. Each day has a purpose of its own, and this is something we seem to have lost in an age where each day seems to be like any other.

If necessary, Mum would alter her timetable and I don't remember her feeling guilty about it, but she preferred to keep to her regular routine. It says something to me about sharing a special time regularly with God. Having a time to pray and read my Bible, without it becoming legalistic or obsessive, has brought me reassurance and security.

I'm sure God understands those who are unable to do this each day, and does not judge them. However, I do think that we are the ones who miss out the most when we rush through our day without acknowledging him.

THE SECRET

I met God in the morning
When my day was at its best,
And his Presence came like sunrise,
Like a glory in my breast.

All day long the Presence lingered,
All day long he stayed with me,
And we sailed in perfect calmness
O'er a very troubled sea.

Other ships were blown and battered,
Other ships were sore distressed,
But the winds that seemed to drive them
Brought to us peace and rest.

But I thought of other moorings,
With a keen remorse of mind,
When I too had loosed the moorings,
With the Presence left behind.

So I think I know the secret.
Learned from many a troubled way:
You must seek him in the morning
If you want him through the day!

Ralph Spaulding Cushman

Mother Nature

My mother was a keen gardener and took great delight in making our garden beautiful. She grew all the bedding plants from seeds each spring and laboriously pricked them out. She encouraged me to do the same, and when I was tiny she gave me a small piece of ground. I grew in it the simplest and easiest of things such as radishes and nasturtiums and I edged it all around with shells collected on holiday from cold beaches in the north-east of England. I was proud of my garden and patiently tended and watered it. In fascination, I watched the worms and beetles I had disturbed. What did it feel like, I wondered, to be a slug or an earwig? Discovering God's creation could keep me occupied for hours.

> He who owns a garden,
> However small it be,
> Whose hands have planted in it
> Flower or bush or tree,
> He who watches patiently
> The growth from nurtured sod,
> Who thrills at newly opened bloom
> Is very close to God.

> *Katherine Edelman*

Frequently asked questions

I'm always full of questions. I suppose I learnt to query things from an early age because my parents encouraged it, and because I was aware of the conflict between my close relatives regarding the nature of God. My mother was quite angry with him. Her father, a schoolteacher of the strictest kind, had convinced her that God was a fierce old man with a big stick poised ready to strike her for the smallest misdemeanour. She saw him as cruel and judgmental, and I think she held him responsible for the cot death of her beloved first son Kenneth at the age of six weeks.

My father, a gentle kindly man, was unsure whether there was a God at all, although I know he searched diligently for faith. My brother had a strong and quiet relationship with the Lord, but later in life this was tested by bouts of severe depression. My granny loved and trusted God without question. It was an interesting family group in which to be raised spiritually speaking, but I think the sheer Christian example of love and kindness on all their parts helped lead me to a strong belief in – and, yes, fear of – God. Fear, that is, as in the Old Testament sense of *awe*.

Perhaps it's true to say that people often fall into the category of being really angry with God or being afraid of him. Anger and fear are two things that God is always trying to counterbalance because I don't believe God wants us to do anything but love him. It's also true to say that he does not object to our questions. In fact, the Bible encourages us to question and enquire. We only have to look at the Psalms:

33

How much longer will you forget me, Lord? For ever?
How much longer will you hide yourself from me?
How long must I endure trouble?
How long will sorrow fill my heart day and night?
How long will my enemies triumph over me?

Look at me, O Lord my God, and answer me.
Restore my strength; don't let me die.
Don't let my enemies say, 'We have defeated him.'
Don't let them gloat over my downfall.

I rely on your constant love;
I will be glad, because you will rescue me.
I will sing to you, O Lord, because you have been good to me.

Psalm 13

God listens

I suppose the desire to say my prayers on a regular basis came initially from the teaching I received at my Church of England school. It was a discipline that I soon extended by not just saying my prayers, but writing them down too. I had a little red exercise book and methodically wrote down prayers that I had composed. Looking back on this, I must admit I was a sickeningly pious child.

Prayer was a vital and necessary part of my life in my early teenage years too and yet something I totally abandoned in later life. How I got through without it I shall never know, but I am convinced it would have been a better journey for me had I kept my prayer life going. Now it is more important to me than ever before, and I don't feel 'goody-goody' when talking to God, just grateful that I am able to chat to him, knowing he listens.

THE PRAYER

Wilt thou not visit me?
The plant beside me feels thy gentle dew,
And every blade of grass I see
From thy deep earth its quickening moisture drew.

Wilt thou not visit me?
Thy morning calls on me with cheering tone;
And every hill and tree
Lend but one voice – the voice of thee alone.

Come for I need thy love,
More than the flower the dew or grass the rain;
Come, gentle as thy holy dove;
And let me in thy sight rejoice to live again.

I will not hide from them
When thy storms come, though fierce may be their wrath,
    but bow with leafy stem, and strengthened follow on
    thy chosen path.

Yes thou wilt visit me:
Nor plant nor tree thine eye delights so well,
As, when from sin set free,
My spirit loves with thine in peace to dwell.

James Very

All in a day's work

Dad was part of a family business. Although its main trade was haulage, it seemed as if he was involved in almost any task needed within our little community. The company made bricks, were responsible for building most of the houses in the village, and even doubled as family undertakers.

Dad's skill as a carpenter came in extremely useful when it came to making the coffins, and I watched fascinated as he dovetailed each joint perfectly in its place. He was a true craftsman.

I knew when Dad was about to go to a funeral because he appeared in our hallway wearing his immaculate tailcoat. I watched as he carefully removed his top hat from its velvet-lined box, brushed it until it was smooth and silky, and placed it carefully on his head with a wink in my direction.

One day when he returned I met him at the front door and I asked, 'Daddy, was it very sad?'

'It wasn't too sad, Darling,' was his reply, 'because it was an old person's funeral and we all have to die one day.'

If it had been a child's funeral, he came home really upset. I expect it brought back all the old pain of his first child's death. He told me that their souls would go to heaven, which made me feel comforted. I hope it comforted him too.

In Victorian times infant death was common. This hymn seems sentimental now, but my father said it was often sung at the funeral of a child, even in the thirties.

There's a Friend for little children
above the bright blue sky,
a Friend who never changes,
whose love will never die;
our earthly friends may fail us,
and change with changing years,
this Friend is always worthy
of that dear Name he bears.

There's a home for little children
above the bright blue sky,
where Jesus reigns in glory,
a home of peace and joy;
no home on earth is like it,
nor can with it compare;
for every one is happy
nor could be happier there.

There's a crown for little children
above the bright blue sky,
and all who look for Jesus
shall wear it by and by;
a crown of brightest glory,
which he will then bestow
on those who found his favour
and loved his Name below.

Albert Midlane

Heaven beckons

The fact that my father was the village undertaker didn't bother me at all. As far as I was concerned, I wasn't going to die. I had determined in my mind that I was going to live for ever. It was a terrific shock when my brother told me that I really would die one day, and that there was no escape, because everybody did eventually.

It wasn't until my fluffy black and white pet rabbit actually demonstrated this fact that the full awareness of death finally came home to me. Having gone out to feed him one morning, I discovered the poor thing with the guillotine-type door having come down on his head. I rushed into the kitchen shouting, 'Mummy, there's something wrong with my rabbit.' Of course he was as stiff as a piece of wood because he had been there all night. Now I really understood what 'dead' meant.

I was, and still am, afraid of the pain, but not of the passing. I believe that there is more to our lives than just the earthly part, and feel sure that our lives on earth are a preparation for something mystical and wonderful beyond.

A SONG OF LIVING

Because I have loved life, I shall have no sorrow to die.
I have sent up my gladness on wings, to be lost in the
blue of the sky.
I have run and leaped with the rain, I have taken wind
to my breast.
My cheek like a drowsy child to the face of the earth I
have pressed.
Because I have loved life, I shall have no sorrow to die.

I have kissed young Love on the lips, I have heard his
song to the end.
I have struck my hand like a seal in the loyal hand of a
friend.
I have known the peace of heaven, the comfort of work
done well.
I have longed for death in the darkness and risen alive
out of hell.
Because I have loved life, I shall have no sorrow to die.

I give a share of my soul to the world where my course
is run
I know that another shall finish the task I must leave
undone.
I know that no flower, nor flint was in vain on the path
I trod.
As one looks on a face through a window, through life I
have looked on God.
Because I have loved life, I shall have no sorrow to die.

Amelia Josephine Burr

Keeping the memory

Sacriston, where I was born and lived until I was nine years old, was a small mining village on the outskirts of Durham. They still had their own 'knocker-upper' as he was called. There were a lot of miners living in our street and a little back lane ran up the rear of the long strip terrace of houses. About 4 a.m. each morning a man would walk up this back alley banging on the back doors of the miners' houses as he went to wake them up, and so ensure the pit got its full complement of workers for the early shift.

If the pit wasn't working for any particular reason – perhaps the machinery was being repaired – this man would come up the back road and shout like a town crier, 'All pits idle the 'morn!' He bellowed so loudly that it woke up everyone in the street, including me. This was just part of everyday life in Sacriston.

The miners were extremely important to the life and prosperity of the village – after all, they *were* the village. *Whellan's 1894 Directory of County Durham* says that the Sacriston and Charlaw collieries were owned by Messrs Hunter and Elliott: 'The output of the Charlaw pit is about 500 tons per day, and the number of hands employed is 300. The Sacriston is expected shortly to be in full operation, when the output is estimated at 1,000 tons per day, and the number employed at 600.'

Mining has always been a very dangerous job and many miners were killed over the years. Here are some excerpts from the Sacriston Colliery memoriam:

Cornell, Charles, 01 Nov 1909, aged 57, Hewer. This case was purely accidental. He was hewing in a bord, where the face had been nicked on the left side, when a piece of coal, weighing from one to two tons, came away from a 'back' and fastened him against a prop. The place was properly timbered, and, but for the 'back', which prior to the occurrence was invisible, the accident would not have happened.

McCormack, Thomas, 16 Nov 1903, aged 52, Hewer. Drowned by an inrush of water into their working places.

Stephenson, Joseph Birtley, 23 Aug 1923, aged 47. Shaftman, accidentally killed while taking down baulks of timber down to the Brass Thill seam; he and another man had removed three baulks from the top of the cage, but as they took off the fourth, Stephenson noticed it was catching, and as he went to ease it, he slipped and fell down the shaft, landing on another cage 78 feet below.

It is fitting that Sacriston Colliery still keeps a list of those who died while serving us down the mines as a memorial.

THE EXPLOSION

On the day of the explosion
Shadows pointed towards the pithead:
In the sun the slagheap slept.

Down the lane came men in pitboots
Coughing oath-edged talk and pipe-smoke,
Shouldering off the freshened silence.

One chased after rabbits; lost them;
Came back with a nest of lark's eggs;
Showed them, lodged them in the grasses.

So they passed in beards and moleskins,
Fathers, brothers, nicknames, laughter,
Through the tall gates standing open.

At noon, there came a tremor; cows
Stopped chewing for a second; sun,
Scarfed as in a heat-haze, dimmed.

The dead go on before us, they
Are sitting in God's house in comfort,
We shall see them face to face –

Plain as lettering in the chapels
It was said, and for a second
Wives saw men of the explosion

Larger than in life they managed –
Gold as on a coin, or walking
Somehow from the sun towards them,

One showing the eggs unbroken.

Philip Larkin

Pride in your work

Mum was a very hard worker, and very houseproud. A lot of physical energy and drive was encapsulated in her small body as she kept our three-bedroom house immaculate. Cooking, cleaning, ironing. She never stopped. With a tin of polish at the ready, she would buff up everything from the lino in the kitchen to the two leather chairs in the front room. She had the radio on all day as she cleaned the windows, washed the curtains, and scrubbed the doorstep until everything was spotless. A side benefit for me was being able to dance about and learn the words to all the songs of the day.

One day Mother took all the coal out of the coal house in our back garden, whitewashed the coal house, and put all the coal back again. She was such a bundle of energy that she just didn't know how to use it up, and could keep going from dawn to dusk.

I never saw her sitting down empty handed. Even on a day trip to the coast she would sit on the beach knitting or embroidering a tablecloth. If I ever want to conjure up a picture of my early childhood, it is of my mother pegging out the washing outside the rear of our house. The washing line was strung across the back lane and I watched as the wind puffed out the white sheets against a northern sky.

The problem came when the coal was delivered. To avoid the washing getting covered in coal dust from the lorries, the ladies in our street would have to take all their washing in, and then hang it all out again once the delivery had been made.

Later, when we moved to the farm, she joined in the farm work – feeding the hens, helping in the hayfields, and cooking huge meals for the men on threshing day. It was the pride that Mum took in her work that I respected. Nothing was done half-heartedly.

I think her strict work ethic rubbed off on me. I never feel a day is satisfactory or complete without achieving something. Even when I'm on holiday I take work with me – a script to read, letters to answer, a piece of writing to be completed. Once on holiday with the children, I wrote stories for them and read them at bedtime. They were eventually turned into a book and I read them on the *Jackanory* television series.

I recognise that this almost manic need to work is not necessarily a good thing, and that making the most of Sunday as a day of rest is very important. What do they say about 'All work and no play . . .'? Perhaps I feel that if I work hard, then everything will be all right:

> Once I've cleaned this house up properly,
> I honestly think I'll get somewhere.
> Once I've pulled out every single piece of furniture and
>   used an abrasive cloth with strong stuff on it,
> I think I shall come to grips with the rest of my life.
> Once I've put everything into separate piles, each
>   containing the same sort of thing (if you know
>   what I mean)
> I think I'll manage.
> Once I've written a list that includes absolutely
>   everything,
> I think the whole business will seem very much clearer.
> Once I've had time to work slowly from one item to
>   another,
> I'm sure things will change.
> Once I've eaten sensibly for more than a week and a
>   half,
> Once I've sorted out the things that are my fault,
> Once I've sorted out the things that are not my fault,

Once I've spent a little more time reading useful
    books,
Being with people I like,
Going to pottery classes,
Getting out into the air, making bread,
Drinking less,
Drinking more, going to the theatre, adopting a Third-
    World child,
Eating free-range eggs,
And writing long letters,
Once I've pulled
Every single piece of furniture *right out*,
And cleaned this house up properly,
Once I've become somebody else . . .
I honestly think I'll get somewhere.

Adrian Plass

Whiter than snow

My ancestors were widely known in Sacriston. The Sacriston Motor Company was part of the Craig family business, as was building in the area. Alan Craig was responsible for haulage; Douglas Craig for street kerbs; George Craig for sand and gravel. One of the many streets was called 'Craiglands' and it survives to this day.

Our own house was farther up the hill situated in a row of thirty terraced houses stretching in a gentle curve. Although the horizontal incline was mild, the vertical one was not, and it took some breath to get from the bottom of our street to our house at the top of Findon hill where the village suddenly stopped.

Each room had a coal fire, and the one in our bedroom was lit whenever we were ill in bed. It was so comforting to be tucked up with the glow of the hot embers playing on the ceiling. It was really snug, which was just as well because I seemed to catch all the usual childhood ailments.

One particular winter was very severe – 1941 I think it was. The snow fell for days. With the white drifts piling higher and higher, the village was cut off for a while until the snowplough came to rescue us. Allistair and I played in the freezing snow that was now four or five feet high for several days, and as a result we both suffered chills. I went on to develop pleurisy, and remained in my bed for weeks.

I think the fun of romping with Allistair in the snow was worth it, although it was quite scary. He was brilliant at inventing orange box vehicles and I always succumbed to being the test driver. Consequently I sat on the wobbly wooden sledge at the top of the hill in the back lane and as Allistair pushed me

I screamed in terror as I slid down the hill, gaining momentum all the way. Allistair stood at the top laughing and laughing. Brothers are like that!

He caught up with me at the bottom and pulled me out of a drift. Swapping his warm, dry gloves for my cold wet ones was his way of making amends, I suppose.

When it is newly fallen, snow is one of God's most beautiful creations, a miracle of purity and perfection. It's amazing to think that those great drifts are formed by separate snowflakes.

TO A SNOWFLAKE

What heart could have thought you? –
Past our devisal
(O filigree petal!)
Fashioned so purely,
Fragilely, surely,
From what Paradisal
Imagineless metal,
Too costly for cost?
Who hammered you, wrought you,
From argentine vapour? –
God was my shaper.
Passing surmisal,
He hammered, He wrought me,
From curled silver vapour,
To lust of His mind: –
Though could'st not have thought me!
So purely, so palely,
Timely, surely
Mightily, fraily,

Insculped and embossed,
With His hammer of wind,
And his graver of frost.

Francis Thompson

Don't mention the war

I boarded at my school during the war because my parents were worried about me travelling under the threat of being bombed. Oddly enough, there were several air raids that came over Durham. I can't imagine the Nazis were bombing Durham – it's more likely that they were focused on more vital targets nearby, but on their way home they would drop odd bombs here and there.

One night the warning siren went off and all we boarders ran down into the basement. We huddled together in fear. The sound was simply terrifying and the whole building shook. For the first time I became aware of something that could really hurt or even kill me. Thankfully, the old building stood firm and protected us from the blast and we all came out frightened but alive.

Here is a wonderful prayer by Valerie M. Boggess. It helps remind me day by day that I have nothing to fear:

I seek Thy protection over my life this night. Shelter me from the storm, O Lord. Give voice to my ears and let me hear Thy ways, O Lord. 'I am power and might. I am the Lord, your God. I am the storm clouds, the night skies all aglow with lightning that echoes from above. I am one season changing into another. I am autumn's end transforming before your eyes into winter's call. Be not afraid for I am with you. Trust in Me and I shall shelter you from the storms of life. I am omnipresent in all that you see. I am the tall majestic pine trees that upwardly reach in higher places. I am the winds that move throughout this night. My peace, I give to thee. Trust in Me and know that I am God. My hand I hold over thee this night. I am the shelter from the storms of life. Though the tempests of this storm rage this night, in morn shall appear the newness of a new day. The sun shall shine and the clouds shall clear the sky. The rains shall cease. Learn to trust in Me and be not afraid. I am in full control. My mighty hand alone balances all of my creation. I am the Lord, your God.' I am so moved by Thy Presence, O Lord. In all that I see this night, I give praise to the Creator of it all. The storms may rage and the tempests may be high, yet my God is here. He knows His own and they are called by name. This night I give Thee praise and worthy are Your ways, O Lord.

The Observer Corps

'George, come in or you'll be killed!' I heard my mother shout at my dad.

At the sound of the air-raid siren I had run from our house down to the shelter that Daddy had built us at the bottom of the garden. I could see the planes and the tracer bullets going over our heads as the dogfight raged. I was terrified as I ran with my mum and brother, but, strangely, my dad found it all extremely exciting. Much to my mum's discomfiture, Dad stayed outside the shelter with his tin hat on, staring up at the glowing sky. He was in the Observer Corps, and although he was not on duty he was absorbed in watching the planes and their manoeuvres. His curiosity and interest rendered him fearless.

Thank goodness our heavenly Father isn't afraid of anything. Sometimes we imagine that the battle between good and evil is an equal one, but it isn't. God is a billion times more powerful, though Satan does his best to convince us otherwise!

> The one whose faith is focussed on God,
> Who finds his security in Him,
> Does not have to live in fear.
> He is not left untouched
> By the tempests of this life,
> And he may be wounded
> By the onslaughts of evil,
> But his great God does not leave him
> To suffer these things alone.
> The Lord cares for His own and delivers him

Even in the midst of the conflicts
That plague him.

If God is truly your God,
You do not have to be afraid
Of the enemy that threatens
Or the affliction that lays you low.
Men all about may fall,
Never to rise again,
But the Lord is by your side
To raise you to your feet
And to lead you to ultimate victory.

Even the ministering spirits of His invisible world
Are watching over you.
They will not allow anything to hurt you
Except by God's loving permission
And through his eternal concern.
Our loving God has promised it:
'Because My child loves Me,
I will never let him go.
I shall feel the pain of his wounds
And bear his hurt
And shall transform that which is ugly
Into that which enriches and blesses.
And when he cries out in agony,
I shall hear and answer him.
I will be close to him and will deliver him,
And I will grant him eternal life.'

Leslie F. Brandt

Before you ask

During the war many people owned garments called siren suits. They helped keep you warm when you had to leave your cosy bed for the air-raid shelter in the middle of the night. The suit consisted of an all-in-one woollen garment complete with legs that you stepped into and zipped up to the neck. Winston Churchill was often seen wearing one.

We didn't have enough clothes coupons to get me a siren suit, but my dad was determined that I would have one. From somewhere, he found an old woollen dressing gown. He cut out the shape of a siren suit and sewed it together, complete with buttons. I was so proud wearing it. It was something I really wanted, yet I never needed to ask my father – he already knew.

Would any of you who are fathers give your son a snake when he asks for a fish? Or would you give him a scorpion when he asks for an egg? Bad as you are, you know how to give good things to your children. How much more, then, will the Father in heaven give the Holy Spirit to those who ask him.

Luke 11:9–12

A place of escape

The need to escape from the overhead madness of the bombers must have been at the top of my parents' priority list. Although evacuation was out of the question as far as we were concerned, Dad quickly came up with an alternative.

Choosing a quiet spot far away from the Luftwaffe flight paths into Durham and Newcastle, Dad prepared a country haven of our own. Set among the bracken and heathland of a friend's farm, the little wooden cottage was hand-built by him within a few weeks, and named Bracken Brae. Standing on stilts to keep it from the damp, the house had two bedrooms, a living room, and even a verandah.

The ten-mile journey meant it was close enough from home to get to easily, but far enough from the bombs to be safe. Mum and Dad had even built a rockery down the hill from where the little timber cottage stood. The flowers seemed to greet us every time Friday evening came for the regular great escape, and we relaxed here with a sense of safety.

Several months later we packed the car on a Friday as usual, climbed in, and began the short journey cross-country to our regular bolthole. As we bumped along the uneven surface of the farm track, we suddenly saw something that made our hearts stop. For there, lying right in the middle of our garden, was an incendiary bomb with tail plate pointing to the sky.

A stray Luftwaffe must have decided to ditch its unused load on to the surrounding countryside, and our haven in the middle of nowhere had been the target. My parents were staggered as they imagined that this would be the one place that we would be safe. Who would bother to bomb a hillside covered with bracken?

We were all speechless, but with an unexploded bomb in the vicinity, it wasn't a good idea to hang around, so we returned home. The bomb was later defused and removed by the local air-raid warden, but until the war was over, our weekends there were never quite the same again.

I'm glad that in God I do find a secure haven no matter what bombshells life can throw at me. I just have to keep reminding myself of this and believing it!

> O God, our help in ages past,
> Our hope for years to come,
> Our shelter from the stormy blast,
> And our eternal home.
>
> Beneath the shadow of your throne
> Your people live secure;
> Sufficient is your arm alone,
> and our defence is sure.
>
> O God, our help in ages past,
> Our hope for years to come,
> Be our defence while life shall last,
> And our eternal home!
>
> *Isaac Watts*

My little doll

Daddy was always making things. He made my cot when I was born and painted it pink. He also made me a little doll. He was modernising our house and he sawed off the round ball from the newel post on the staircase. He carved a face on it and it became a doll's head. Then he tied a piece of brightly coloured cloth around its base to create the finished doll. It was just a ball with a piece of cloth round it, but I loved it. She soon became my favourite plaything.

There was a deep ditch running down the side of the road near our house. In wet weather a narrow stream ran through it and lush green plants grew on its banks. I often took my dolly there and floated her down the little stream. She was a good swimmer! It was a simple, but wonderful, gift from my father, and when I think back my doll reminds me how our heavenly Father is a giver too. I often have to remind myself with these words sent to me by a friend:

1 God wants to give us gifts. He has a list a mile long.
2 God wants to give his gifts to everyone. Nobody is left out.
3 God's gifts cannot be bought. No amount of money or sacrifice will do.
4 God's gifts are unconditional. There are no strings attached.

Let's enjoy God's gifts to us this day:

He continued this subject with his disciples. 'Don't fuss about what's on the table at mealtimes or if the clothes in your closet are in fashion. There is far more to your inner life than the food you put in your stomach, more to your outer appearance than the clothes you hang on your body. Look at the ravens, free and unfettered, not tied down to a job description, carefree in the care of God. And you count far more.

'Has anyone by fussing before the mirror ever gotten taller by so much as an inch? If fussing can't even do that, why fuss at all? Walk into the fields and look at the wildflowers. They don't fuss with their appearance – but have you ever seen colour and design quite like it? The ten best-dressed men and women in the country look shabby alongside them. If God gives such attention to the wildflowers, most of them never even seen, don't you think he'll attend to you, take pride in you, do his best for you?

'What I'm trying to do here is get you to relax, not be so preoccupied with *getting* so you can respond to God's *giving*. People who don't know God and the way he works fuss over these things, but you know both God and how he works. Steep yourself in God-reality, God-initiative, God-provisions. You'll find all your everyday human concerns will be met. Don't be afraid of missing out. You're my dearest friends! The Father wants to give you the very kingdom itself.'

Luke 12:22–31, The Message

Connecting the future
with the past

Recently my elder son Alaster was playing in the Royal Ballet Symphonia at a theatre near Durham. Alaster, who takes great interest in family history, decided to drive over to Butsfield to see if anything of our little holiday home had survived.

He found the area I described to him quite easily. Sadly, the cottage Daddy had built was now just a pile of firewood and broken glass, but Alaster managed to pluck a piece of metal from the rubble. It was an old calor gas wall lamp. He took it home and spent hours removing the rust and polishing it until it shone. He wired it up for electricity and found a carpenter he knew to make a polished wooden base for it. When Alaster presented it to me at Christmas I was astounded and touched. He had finished the gift with an engraved plaque which read 'From Bracken Brae'. That was the name my mother had given the cottage. The lamp sits on my desk, and every time I touch it I think of how I have known this lamp since I was a small child.

I am so grateful to Alaster for the time and trouble he took to give me such a lasting token of the happy times I spent in my childhood.

MEMORIES KEEP THOSE WE LOVE
CLOSE TO US FOREVER

Hold fast to your memories,
to all of the cherished moments
of the past,
to the blessings and the laughter,
the joys and the celebrations,
the sorrow and the tears.
They all add up to a treasure
of fond yesterdays
that you shared and spent together,
and they keep the one you loved
close to you in spirit and thought.

The special moments
and memories in your life
will never change.
They will always be in your heart,
today and forevermore.

Linda E. Knight

The psalmist said it this way:

I will remember your miracles of long ago. I will
consider all your works and meditate on all
your mighty deeds.

Psalm 77:11, 12

Patience is a virtue

During my early schooling my parents sent me to elocution classes with an inspired teacher called Margaret Marshall who lived in Durham City. She was a great encourager and opened up the doors of drama and literature to me.

When my parents allowed it, I went to Darlington Repertory Theatre at least twice a week. This was paradise to me. Making sure I had done my homework, I would then have to seriously plead with my parents for the money to buy a seat for one of the theatre's varied productions. It was quite expensive, especially when I was going several times a week.

The theatre was run by an actor called Charles Simon. One day my dad took me to the stage door so that he could introduce me. 'If you ever have any parts for a young girl, Wendy would be willing to learn,' he said.

'I'll bear her in mind,' Charles replied.

True to his word, I was summoned to the theatre several times to play small parts, and I just adored it. It was weekly rep, which meant the other actors were rehearsing one play during the day and performing another at night. They were pretty exhausted, so it can't have helped when this awful precocious child bounced in and bawled 'I wish we did a matinee every day!' I bet they could have strangled me.

Although the following sounds as though it has been written by 'Little Mary Sunshine', I have found this good advice, and quite honestly I don't think you can fault it:

Believe in your heart that something wonderful is about to happen.

Love your life.

Believe in your own powers, and your own potential.

Wake every morning with the awe of just being alive.

Discover each day the magnificent beauty in the world.

Explore and embrace life in yourself and in everyone you see each day.

Reach within to find your own special-ness.

Let those who love you help you.

Look with hope to the horizon of today, for today is all we truly have.

Let a little sunshine out, as well as in.

Create your own rainbows, be open to all your possibilities and always believe in miracles. Always believe in miracles.

Terry Mara

A little glimpse of heaven

When I was about thirteen we moved to a farm in a small Yorkshire village called Picton, near Yarm-on-Tees. My brother had decided he wanted to make farming his career, so my father sent him to be trained as a farm manager and bought the farm for him to run. My father was wonderfully kind to his children and provided us with every opportunity to succeed in life.

Life on the farm was a time of great spiritual awakening for me. I felt very close to God as I wandered through the fields, delighted and amazed at the beauty of creation. I loved the dear familiar animals, the gentle-eyed cows with their sweet grassy breath, the pigs joyfully rootling about in the sty surrounded by pink squealing piglets. There were dogs and cats to talk to, and my father bought me a pony. He was a chestnut with a golden mane and tail, and he went under the uninspired name of 'Shorty'.

There was a newly planted copse a couple of fields away from the house. I was wandering along its dewy paths one morning, and as I went I felt myself drifting into a dream-like state of pure ecstasy. Bursts of birdsong, shafts of sunlight through dew-spangled branches, and the sharp perfume of pine needles all mingled and wove a special magic. All was a'shimmer and a'glimmer. It was a breathtaking sensation, so potent that I shall never forget it.

Such a feeling of ecstasy has only touched me once since then. It was when I was walking through a blossoming cherry orchard many years later, after I had just returned to my faith. As the petals drifted like snow on to the lush grass, I could hardly draw breath, so close did I feel God's presence. Was it a glimpse of heaven? I've often wondered.

Of the many poets who have written about nature, I believe Gerard Manley Hopkins to be one who successfully describes God's creation and manages to embrace its spiritual qualities as well:

PIED BEAUTY

Glory be to God for dappled things –
For skies of couple-colour as a brindled cow;
For rose-moles all in stipple upon trout that swim;
Fresh-firecoal chestnut-falls; finches' wings;
Landscape plotted and pieced – fold, fallow and plough;
And all trades, their gear and tackle and trim.
All things counter, original, spare, strange;
Whatever is fickle, freckled (who knows how?)
With swift, slow; sweet, sour, adazzle, dim;
He fathers-forth whose beauty is past change:
Praise him.

Gerard Manley Hopkins

I was excited to see that Theodore Brakel, a Dutch Pietist in the seventeenth century, seems to have had a similar experience:

I was . . . transported into such a state of joy and my thoughts were so drawn upward that, seeing God with the eyes of my soul, I felt one with him. I felt myself transported into God's being and at the same time I was so filled with joy, peace, and sweetness, that I cannot express it. With my spirit I was entirely in heaven for two or three days.

The audition

The turning point from school play and bit parts at Darlington to something much more serious came when Middlesbrough Little Theatre were doing a special production for the Festival of Britain. They agreed on Hamlet. I was attending Yarm Grammar School then, and the headmistress, Miss Manners, was a very good actor. She taught French and Scripture in the most exciting and enlightened way. This lovely tall lady became such an encouragement to me when she noticed my desire to perform, and persuaded me to audition for this new production of Hamlet.

Lady Crathorne, a governess of the school, had seen me in several school productions and was also determined that I should audition. Both women talked to my parents, inspired and instructed me in the art of displaying my skills, and prepared me for the audition. My parents were thoroughly supportive, and I had a great sense that no matter how much my desire to be in the theatre worried them, they simply wanted the best for me.

Now properly prepared to face the audition panel, I recognised inside me a mixture of deep fear and excitement as I waited to be called in to strut my stuff.

'Please come this way, Wendy,' came the disembodied voice as the door creaked open. Stepping inside, I kept my composure, took a firm and confident position on the floor and began:

I shall the effect of this good lesson keep.
As watchmen to my heart.
But, good my brother, do not, as some ungracious
    pastors do,
Show me the steep and thorny way to heaven;
Whiles, like a puffed and reckless libertine,
Himself the primrose path of dalliance treads,
And recks not his own rede.

I performed with the combined coaxing of Miss Manners and my observation and impersonation of my hero Jean Simmonds. After all, I knew the part of Ophelia so well because I had seen the film version of Hamlet with Laurence Olivier at least twelve times.

Later that week, Miss Manners called me into her office to say that I had been successful in my attempt. I was thrilled to have been given the part. Here was I about to embark on playing one of the most favoured roles in the theatre, and I was still only a teenager. Surrounded by so much encouragement, I was on my way. Encouragement is so important in our lives:

Let us not give up meeting together, as some are in the habit of doing, but let us encourage one another – and all the more as you see the Day approaching.

Hebrews 10:25, NIV

Faith alongside

The next step of my career was attending the Central School of Speech Training and Dramatic Art in London. I was still under the watchful eye of Lady Crathorne, who arranged my accommodation at the Three Arts Club. This was a sort of hostel for women involved in drama, music and dance. Centrally placed in Great Cumberland Place, just by Marble Arch, it was perfectly positioned for me to simply walk across Hyde Park to the Royal Albert Hall where the Central School was. It provided the perfect, secure place to begin my initiation into city life.

I brought my faith with me to London, and for some while attended church with all my usual zeal. Westminster Chapel was a firm favourite, with its massive congregation of several hundred, and its exciting preachers, like Martin Lloyd-Jones. I always left feeling inspired.

Other individuals inspired me too. Derek Elphinstone was an actor who led Bible Studies at his mews house in Paddington. Some friends had taken me along to his group where we spent most of the time sitting around, drinking tea and chatting. It was good to be able to discuss our faith in the relaxed and informal atmosphere that a church could not provide. This led to an invitation from Derek to a weekend retreat at a place called Rose Hill. It was here that for the first time I gave my personal testimony of what God had done in my life.

I was also aware, however, of how 'worldly' I was becoming. My faith was being stretched between what I had been taught, and what everybody appeared to be doing. Life in London was exciting and I wanted to join in:

I do not understand what I do; for I don't do what I would like to do, but instead I do what I hate . . . when I want to do what is good, what is evil is the only choice I have. My inner being delights in the law of God. But I see a different law at work in my body – a law that fights against the law which my mind approves of. It makes me a prisoner to the law of sin which is at work in my body. What an unhappy man I am! Who will rescue me from this body that is taking me to death? Thanks be to God, who does this through our Lord Jesus Christ!

St Paul, speaking in Romans 7:15–25

Love at first sight

The famous saying in showbusiness that 'It's not what you know, it's who you know' is quite accurate. Often the best way to achieve this is through the intense socialising that goes on in the profession. Performers love to spend their time with their colleagues – in some ways it's like being part of an exclusive club, but really it's more a case of having so much in common. I loved the parties. It was at one of these that I met Jack.

The telephone rang and on the other end was my best friend, Anne. We met when we were both working at Middlesbrough Little Theatre, and we often got together for coffee and a chat.

This particular evening she'd invited me to a party at Bobby Howes's flat. He was the famous musical star and father of Sally Anne Howes.

I arranged to meet her at my bed-sit and we'd walk across the park together to collect her escort, Jack. As we neared the appointed place, Anne said, 'That's him. That's Jack.'

I looked and saw him standing on the steps of St George's Hospital with a boxer dog at his feet. I instinctively thought, 'What a lovely man.' He was standing firmly on both feet and looking straight out at the passing traffic. He looked solid and reliable, perhaps reminding me a little of my dad. I felt immediately that he was somebody I could trust.

I really fell for this mysterious man that night, and was relieved to find out a few days later that his relationship with Anne wasn't serious. It was just a friendship. Jack and I began going out together and all my feelings about him were justified.

It lies not in our power to love or hate,
For will in us is overruled by fate.
When two are stripped, long ere the course begin,
We wish that one should love, the other win;
And one especially do we affect
Of two gold ingots, like in each respect:
The reason no man knows, let it suffice,
What we behold is censured by our eyes.
Where both deliberate, the love is slight:
Who ever loved, that loved not at first sight?

Christopher Marlowe

Music — food of love

Jack was also hard at work at this time. He was an accomplished and successful trombonist who played regularly with all the Big Bands of the day, including the Ted Heath Band. When I went to see him play with the BBC Big Band at the Aeolian Hall in London one day, I was extremely proud of him. Whenever Jack stood up to play a solo, I was thrilled by his talent as a musician.

I always loved listening to the Ted Heath Band as a teenager, and as I sat listening to the brass section blasting away, I had a clear flashback to my teenage years. My father had taken me down to the shops, and had left the radio on in the car. As I waited for Dad to return, the Ted Heath Band began playing 'Midnight Sun'. A slow and moody tune, this modern jazz piece included the trombone skills of Jack Bentley. He played it so beautifully. Little did I know that a few years later I would be marrying him. Perhaps I was already a little in love.

VALENTINE

My heart has made its mind up
And I'm afraid it's you.
Whatever you've got lined up,
My heart has made its mind up
And if you can't be signed up

This year, next year will do.
My heart has made its mind up
And I'm afraid it's you.

Wendy Cope

Wedding bells

I really wanted a church wedding, but perhaps it was the old recurring feeling of wanting to 'hedge my bets'. I decided that if there was a God, then I wanted his blessing on my marriage. I really believed every word of my vows as I stood before family, friends and colleagues in the packed church.

My heart melted once more as the choir sang 'God Be in My Head' so beautifully. As Jack loved music, it was important to him that we have the best harmonious send-off imaginable, and the choir's a cappella version was outstanding.

We made our exit arm in arm past all the pews crowded with family, friends, singers, actors, dancers and musicians, and emerged from St Columbus's church just as the bells rang. As I had already begun to make a name in the business, hordes of press photographers started to flash away. The car whisked us off to the reception rooms in Park Lane, where we partied on champagne and finger food for the rest of the afternoon. I couldn't have been happier.

The only downside was leaving my own wedding party to perform that night. Exchanging my 1955 wedding dress for an ordinary skirt and jumper in *Mr Kettle and Mrs Moon*, I was soon back on stage at the Duchess Theatre, and in full flow. Right in the middle of the first scene, I suddenly lost the wedding ring that had been placed on my finger a few hours earlier.

'I've lost my wedding ring already!' I hissed at the stage manager in the wings.

Playing the role of Monica Twig, the landlady's daughter, I had slipped the ring off my wedding finger and on to another, as I wasn't supposed to be married.

Using all my powers of concentration to get me through the performance, I tried not to panic. I was incredibly relieved two hours later when one of the stage-crew rushed into my dressing room and handed me the ring. He had found it down the back of the sofa on stage.

I was more than glad that this symbolic piece of gold had been rescued, for I was now able to wear it for our one-night honeymoon at the Savoy Hotel, before rising the following morning for the matinee. Though the wedding and honeymoon were short, I wanted to make sure that my marriage lasted for ever.

> May these vows and this marriage be blessed.
> May it be sweet milk,
> this marriage, like wine and halvah.
> May this marriage offer fruit and shade
> like the date palm.
> May this marriage be full of laughter,
> our every day a day in paradise.
> May this marriage be a sign of compassion,
> a seal of happiness here and hereafter.
> May this marriage have a fair face and a good name,
> an omen as welcome
> as the moon in a clear blue sky.
> I am out of words to describe
> how spirit mingles in this marriage.

Rumi, wedding poem, translated by Kabir Helminski

This song dates from the nineteenth or twentieth Egyptian dynasty (about 1300–1100 BC). It was found written in hieroglyphics on a vase and it talks about a perfect love:

This love is as good
as oil and honey to the throat,
as linen to the body,
as fine garments to the gods,
as incense to worshippers when they enter in,
as the little seal-ring to my finger.

It is like a ripe pear in a man's hand.
It is like the dates we mix with wine.
It is like the seeds the baker adds to bread.

We will be together even when old age comes.
And the days in between
will be food set before us,
dates and honey, bread and wine.

Life and laughter

Jack had come to a time in his life where he felt he'd gone as far as he could with his playing career. He pondered with the idea that the Big Bands might not last much longer. The Beatles were changing popular music, and he felt this was the perfect time to bow out. A career change would also create greater stability between us, he suggested, understanding the problems that are caused by a married couple both away from home in such a demanding profession.

Not wanting to be out on the road any more, he accepted a job with the *Record Mirror* newspaper as a critic and writer, began writing links for several bands, and later added a showbusiness column for the *Sunday Mirror* to his repertoire. He soon became showbusiness editor, and remained with them for more than twenty-five years. Jack was firmly established with the *Sunday Mirror* and a new play was on offer for me.

Man Alive starred the great comedy actor Robertson Hare, and he was a delight to work with as he was so sweet-tempered and unassuming. Jack remained the great enthusiast of all that I did, and had tremendous faith in me right from the word go. He was wonderfully unselfish about my growing success, always gave me every encouragement, and never stood in my way. Jack had two very different careers in his life, and both were very successful, but now he seemed to be saying that it was my turn.

I was just as delighted with the growth in my career, and was pleased to take whatever came along next, hoping it would enhance my reputation, and get me known more. I was not at the point where I could pick and choose, but at least those dreaded auditions were becoming a thing of the past.

A number of theatre plays followed throughout the 1960s, including a season at the Royal Court. This was a particularly rewarding time as the Royal Court under George Devine was producing plays by new and exciting writers and was regarded as *the* place to work. We performed *Epitaph for George Dillon* by John Osborne and Anthony Creighton; *The Sport of My Mad Mother* by Anne Jellicoe; and *A Resounding Tinkle*, one of several hilarious plays by N. F. Simpson. He was a forerunner of the theatre of the absurd, and sparked off such offbeat comedy as *Monty Python*.

I discovered I adored making people laugh. It gave me huge pleasure and was to become a major feature of my career.

This poem by N. F. Simpson demonstrates his use of clichés and absurd situations in his wonderfully zany humour:

ONE OF OUR ST BERNARD DOGS IS MISSING

A moot point
Whether I was going
To make it.
I just had the strength
To ring the bell.

There were monks inside
And every one of them
Eventually
Opened the door.

Oh
He said.
This is a bit of a turn up
He said
For the book.

Opportune
He said
Your arriving at this particular
As it were
Moment.

You're dead right
I said
It was touch and go
Whether I could have managed
To keep going
For very much longer

No
He said
The reason I used the word opportune
Is that
Not to put too fine a point on it
One of our St Bernard Dogs is
Unfortunately
Missing.

Oh dear
I said
Not looking for me I hope.

No
He said
It went for a walk
And got lost in the snow

Dreadful thing
I said
To happen

Yes
He said
It is.

To
Of all creatures
I said
A St Bernard dog
That has devoted
Its entire
Life
To doing good
And helping others

What I was actually thinking
He said
Since you happen to be
In a manner of speaking
Out there already
Is that
If you could
At all
See your way clear
To having a scout
Around
It would save one of us
Having to
If I can so put it
Turn out.

Ah
I said
That would
I suppose
Make a kind of sense

Before you go
He said
If I can find it
You'd better
Here it is
Take this

What is it?
I said

It's a flask
He said
Of brandy.

Ah
I said.

For the dog
He said.

Good thinking
I said.

The drill
He said
When you find it
If you ever do
Is to lie down.

Right
I said
Will do.

Lie down on top of it
He said
To keep it warm
Till help arrives.

This was a week ago, and my hopes are rising all the time. I feel with ever-increasing confidence that once I can safely say that I am within what might be called striking distance of knowing where, within a square mile or two, to start getting down to looking, my troubles are more or less, to all intents and purposes, apart from frostbite, with any luck, and help arrives at long last, God willing, as good as over. It is good to be spurred on with hope.

N. F. Simpson

Brushing God aside

God had already been sidetracked as the world of the theatre took over, and my faith had been slowly eroded. I stopped attending church or reading my Bible, and there never seemed time to pray any more. Jack did not agree with my faith, and so it was particularly difficult to share that part of my life with him.

Sometimes I would stop and wonder what had happened to all my youthful fervour.

'What was all that stuff I used to do? Where did all the singing of hymns and going to church and praying go?' I questioned myself. 'Perhaps it was just something to do with growing up' was the best excuse I could think of.

Although this explanation did not rest easily with me, I got to the point of denying my faith altogether, and deliberately turned my back on all the experiences and understanding I had gained over the years.

God, I decided, was a panacea for people who had nothing much in life. He was for people who were afraid, or were weak.

As far as I was concerned, God was now firmly out in the cold. Soon I didn't even think about him, and had no time for him at all. Except when it suited me, of course. On first nights, I was particularly terrified and I would still pray in the wings before I went on stage. It was more akin to a lucky charm. Like taking out some heavenly insurance policy against anything awful going wrong, I would go through the ritual of locking myself in the backstage loo and reciting the Lord's Prayer. At the grandest theatres in the country and before the most salubrious television shows, there would be Wendy, sitting on the loo, delivering her prayer, as if touching wood. Strangely enough, those gabbled prayers did give me confidence.

The parties were always such fun and I indulged in the revelry of the scene as much as possible. One such party was particularly wild. The alcohol flowed as much as the people who came and went all evening. As I wandered from one end of the room to another I happened to glance out of the window and through it was the sharp outline of a church against the moonlight.

I looked at it and thought, 'Oh my God. What am I doing?'

Something deep within my heart sank, as I felt a longing to be back in my innocent and secure childhood faith. The next morning I had forgotten once more.

THE HOUND OF HEAVEN

I fled him, down the nights and down the days;
I fled him, down the arches of the years;
I fled him, down the labyrinthine ways
Of my own mind; and in the midst of tears
I hid from him, and under running laughter.
Up vistaed hopes I sped;
And shot, precipitated,
Adown Titanic glooms of chasmed fears,
From those strong Feet that followed, followed after.
But with unhurrying chase,
And unperturbed pace,
Deliberate speed, majestic instancy,
They beat – and a Voice beat
More instant than the Feet –
'All things betray thee, who betrayest me'.

Halts by me that footfall:
Is my gloom, after all,
Shade of his hand, outstretched caressingly?
'Ah, fondest, blindest, weakest,
I am he whom thou seekest!
Thou dravest love from thee, who dravest me.'

Francis Thompson

Not in Front of the Children

In some ways I can see how easily my faith was pushed aside and why I stopped meeting with other Christians. There were so many things on offer and, being young, I found them all so exciting. I discovered that if I ignored God for long enough, I soon became hardened to the feeling of living my life without Him.

Fame was beckoning and, after a string of better and better stage parts, Richard Waring, a writer friend of ours, penned a pilot show with me in his mind as the poor old mum who always seemed to fail.

'There's a comedienne lurking in you, Wendy,' Richard said across the dinner table one evening. 'I'd love to bring it out.'

I just smiled and made a silly quip.

'No, really,' he persevered. 'I've an idea for a pilot script that I'd like to write for you.'

'What's it called?' I said.

'*Not in Front of the Children*. What do you think?'

The next few moments of pondering probably changed my life.

'Yes, I'd love to try it.'

I hadn't done a lot of comedy on television before and so approached the new role with some apprehension. I needn't have worried. Richard's writing was so good; it fitted me like a glove. 'I can hear your voice when I'm writing it,' he said. 'I feel you are there when I'm putting it down, and I know what your reactions are going to be.'

The series was rehearsed in a church hall in Chiswick, very handy for me as we lived close by. During rehearsals I found myself looking at the Sunday School notices and pictures pinned up on the walls. It was as if God was in the business of 'nudging' me, but he was never 'pushy'.

Soon after rehearsals started, I began to feel very much at home in Jennifer Corner's skin. It became a comfortable part to play. A slightly daffy character, her wish was always to do her best for her family, but she was naïve and unworldly, which brought all sorts of complications into her life. Part of the success of the series was due to its simplicity. It was just a portrait of happy family life.

We rehearsed on weekday mornings, and went into the studio for a run-through with the cameras on the Saturday. Sunday would be a full dress rehearsal about five o'clock, a quick bite to eat, restoration of make-up, and the final recording on Sunday evening in front of a live audience over a two-hour period. From the very first episode, the laughs from the studio audience came thick and fast. Little did I realise that I was to make myself at home in this role for the following four years. Even further from my imagination was that this pilot and subsequent series would spawn similar situation comedies for the next fifteen years, and soon established me as a household name.

Within a week, the success of the pilot was noted and *Not in Front of the Children* was to span four series with a total of thirty-seven episodes. The last series had seventeen episodes between September 1969 and January 1970. It was very hard work keeping up with it all, but always great fun.

Among all the new-found fame, God was somehow still there in the background. He never abandoned me; he never gave up on me. He just bided his time.

THE GREAT INTRUDER

It is exasperating
To be called
So persistently
When the last thing
We want to do
Is get up
And go
But God
Elects
To keep on haunting
Like some
Holy ghost.

Thomas John Carlisle

Your God, the Lord himself, will be with you.
He will not fail you or abandon you.

Deuteronomy 31:6

The wilderness years

Despite all the years I spent walking away from God, I was constantly reminded of his loving presence. A wedding service. The Salvation Army playing on the street corner. Nativity Plays. After I renewed my faith I wrote the words and music to this carol for busy mums.

THE GOOD NEWS CAROL

I hurry down the high street
My shopping in my hand
I try to hear the carols
From the Sally Army band
Tired of all the hustle
The pushing and the queues
Then all at once I heard it
Good News!

I won't forget that Christmas
The season of goodwill
Is more than work and worry
And shopping bags to fill
For I reached out and touched the baby's hand
I touch it
I touch it still

More cards and wrapping paper
More baubles for the tree
More mince pies in the oven
To please the family
Feeling tired and weary
I have the Christmas blues
When a star shone through the window
Good News!

I won't forget that Christmas
The season of goodwill
Is more than work and worry
And shopping bags to fill
For I reached out and held the baby's hand
I hold it
I hold it still

I wish you Merry Christmas
My heart's so full of joy
Welcome little baby
Welcome darling boy
You came to bring us gladness
You came that we might lose
Our guilt our fear our sadness
Good News!

I won't forget that Christmas
The season of goodwill
Is more than work and worry
And shopping bags to fill
For I reached out and held the Saviour's hand
I hold it
I always will

Wendy Craig

Just a minute

Do you ever ask the question, 'If I only had a minute of my life left, what would I do?'

If I were alone, I would just pray. If I were with my family, I would hug them all and tell them that I love them.

I would like to think that I wouldn't waste those few moments in useless panic or screaming, but be able to put my remaining seconds to good use, but who knows how one would react in such circumstances? Many people have had to face just this situation. With the tsunami and other natural disasters, as well as terrorist attacks, wars and accidents of one kind or another and medical emergencies, it is possible that any one of us might have to be prepared for our lives to end at any time. I think about this possibility because I want to be ready and prepared to meet God. It also reminds me to enjoy life now.

We once came very close to disaster on a flight from Heathrow airport to Nice, though strangely enough I didn't realise how serious it was at the time. As we approached our destination it became apparent that the landing gear had stuck. We were asked to vacate our seats and the cabin crew set about removing them and opening up the floor. The landing gear was then cranked down with what looked like a huge spanner. I was frightened, but had to pretend to be quite nonchalant about it because the boys were with us. Jack was brilliant. Ross asked him, 'What is that man doing?'

'He's winding up the elastic,' was his calm reply.

Thank God we landed safely. This same plane crashed at Nice a few days later with many fatalities.

Our great God is still our Refuge and Strength:
He is ever aware of our problems and fears.
Thus we have no business doubting Him,
Even though the earth is convulsed in tragedy
Or its human masses are threatened
By nuclear annihilation.

God continues to reign as all-wise
And as almighty as ever.
His eternal plan is not cancelled out
By the whims of men
Or the freakish accidents of nature.
Nations will destroy each other;
Civilisations will perish;
The earth itself may one day become
A smoking cinder, but God will not leave us.
He is forever our sure Refuge and Strength.

Just look about you; read the pages of history.
Refresh your flagging spirits with the reminder
Of his great feats throughout the ages.
And you will again hear Him speaking:
'Relax, stop fretting, and
Remember that I am still your God;
I still hold the reins on this world of yours.'

God is here among us:
He continues to be our Refuge and Strength.

Leslie F. Brandt

Parenting isn't for cowards

My sons were both at school during my 'TV Mother' years.

Jack, being fiercely loyal about my work, liked the boys to sit with him to watch the shows when they were aired. Naturally they both became a little fidgety, and indeed Ross once found it upsetting. Blurting out a worried question, 'Mummy, are you here?', he then went on to enquire, 'Then who is that on the television?' Recognising how desperately confused he was, I decided that he should not watch me on television until he was old enough to properly understand. I didn't like watching myself on the box anyway, and so this family arrangement suited the three of us. Jack viewed the series on his own.

As any parent will testify, being a mum or dad is full of joys and woes, and Jack and I struggled to do the right thing. On many occasions I was tempted to pray a parent's prayer just like this one:

> Now I lay me down to sleep,
> I pray my sanity to keep.
> For if some peace I do not find,
> I'm pretty sure I'll lose my mind.
>
> I pray I find a little quiet,
> Far from the daily family riot.
> May I lie back and not have to think
> About what they're stuffing down the sink.

Or who they're with, or where they're at
And what they're doing to the cat.
I pray for time all to myself
(Did something just fall off a shelf?)

To cuddle in my nice, soft bed
(Oh no, another goldfish – dead!)
Some silent moments for goodness' sake
(Did I just hear a window break?)

And that I need not cook or clean
(Well, heck, I've got the right to dream)
Yes, now I lay me down to sleep,
I pray my wits about me keep,
But as I look around I know,
I must have lost them long ago!

Author unknown

God's medicine

Not in Front of the Children came to the end of its natural life in the early part of 1970. I think that everybody connected with the series felt we had done enough. I always feel that there is a stopping time.

However, Thames Television was on the phone to my agent shortly afterwards saying that they would like me to come over to them. I had no hesitation in accepting, as it was a show with two new writers I had not worked with before, Peter Buchanan and Peter Robinson. The character I had played now had a different angle on it altogether. *And Mother Makes Three* enjoyed twenty-six episodes over the next three years, with me playing the part of Sally Harrison, a widow trying to hold down a job and bring up two young sons. My Auntie Flo, played by Valerie Lush, was usually on hand to provide help and hindrance in equal measures. At the end of the series, Sally married widower David Redway, played by Richard Coleman, and a sequel, *And Mother Makes Five*, was born.

This series spanned from 1974 to 1976, and although I knew it was funny, I sometimes wondered how long the viewing public would actually keep watching. The huge viewing figures were telling a different story, though. It was in the top ten listings each week. People still wanted to see it, and television companies still wanted to put money into it. Laughter was big business, and something that I've always believed is that laughter is one of the best medicines available.

Recent medical research shows that adults laugh an average of 15 times each day, but children laugh 125 times a day.

People who regularly exercise their face muscles can expect to delay middle-aged sagging for at least ten years.

Eva Fraser, The Facial Workout Studio

100 laughs a day gives you as much beneficial exercise as 10 minutes of rowing.

Dr William Fry, Stanford Medical School

Laughter increases production of immunoglobulins, antibodies which boost the immune system.

Robert Holden, founder of first NHS Laughter Clinic

Regular laughter permanently lowers your heart rate and blood pressure.

Dr Annette Goodheart, independent laughter therapist

Laughter at the table

When one of the writers for *And Mother Makes Five* became ill, Richard Waring stood in and penned a few episodes. He was then very busy writing another series and could not spare us any more time. So Jack and I suggested that because we knew the characters and situations inside out, we could write an episode ourselves. It worked so well that we wrote quite a few over the next couple of years. Here began our taste for writing television comedy, which would come in even handier later on.

One of the other writers was Carla Lane, who wrote an episode for the last series. After three years of *And Mother Makes Five*, I really did feel that the time for this type of sitcom was over. At least, I pondered, there can't be much more that I could do in such a role. I was proved wrong when Carla Lane approached me with a new idea for a programme called *Butterflies*. I thought the script was special, liked the part that had been created for me, and so it was back to the good old BBC for the next six years. *Butterflies* ran from 1978 to 1983, and I loved every minute of it.

Now famous for my role as a mother in a series of television shows, the funniest moments of *Butterflies* were when my hopeless cooking brought constant consternation from the 'family'. Such lines as 'Must you peer like that?' brought howls of laughter from audiences as my character placed yet another burnt cinder of a dish before them.

'You always peer into the food dishes looking as if you are expecting to come face to face with a nasty accident!' were the sort of lines that I cherished, and that were based on the fact that Carla thought she was no good in the kitchen herself.

Actually that's not true. She's cooked me some delicious meals, all vegetarian of course because of her love for animals.

The burnt food became a sort of hinge point in the series. Horrid food, lumpy custard, steamed puddings that were like rocks, were all part of the everyday menu, and became a running gag. We had a good laugh acting it all out, and encouraged Carla to put some frightful mishap in the show each week.

If Ben, Ria and the boys had bowed their heads before eating the meal, perhaps they would have said something like this:

HYPOCHONDRIAC'S GRACE

Dear Lord, we ask you if you will,
put your blessing on this meal.
We ask you, Father, if it pleases,
protect us from these new diseases.

Please bless the spinach, and the romaine.
And cleanse it of some lurking ptomaine.
God, bless our ice cream and our cola.
Pray it's not teeming with Ebola.

And pray the deli didn't sell us
coleslaw ripe with salmonellas.
We also ask a special blessing;
no botulism in the dressing.

While we regard your higher power,
make sure the devilled eggs aren't sour.
And please, Lord, bless our sirloin tip,
and purge it of E. Coli's grip.

A special blessing on the sherry,
oh Lord, we need no dysentery,
so it not poisons, nor impacts,
or liquefies our lower tracts.

And Lord, make sure no one is able
to get sick and die upon this table.
So bless, Lord, all this food we share.
Insure no deadly virus there.

And once we're full and satiated,
we pray we aren't all contaminated,
and wind up just another toll,
for the Centre for Disease Control.

One last thing, Lord, if it's OK,
Please hold this blessing that we pray.
For all this fear, and all this fright,
has made us lose our appetite.

Amen

Fred Moore

The fickleness of fame

It was *Not in Front of the Children* that quickly launched me into the public domain. When you enter someone's private home via the television on a regular basis it's easy to be seen as public property, and it became increasingly difficult to get out and about without being constantly interrupted by people. Although it was awkward to have my privacy taken away, I always looked on it as a compliment. Shopping was a particular problem as people would always come up and ask questions or request an autograph. I always felt a bit silly signing my name on a scrap of paper standing next to the frozen peas! People were generally very pleasant and kind, however, and it was often a pleasurable experience – it's just that it took so long for me to get the groceries!

I found the most difficult moments were when the family wanted to be able to enjoy a quiet meal together in a restaurant. This was not really possible, and I always felt sorry for Jack and the boys. They didn't get a lot of peace when I was with them in public. One day I decided to do something about it, and actually went to some lengths to create privacy.

We were on holiday in southern France, and although I was sure that no one would notice me so far from home, I decided that I would not take any chances. Jack and I were sitting on the verandah of a restaurant, enjoying some Gallic delicacy, and I had covered my own short fair hair with a long-haired brown wig and donned dark glasses. Suddenly some English people drove by in an open-topped car and shouted across the street:

'Hello, Wendy! Why are you wearing that wig?'

We doubled up with laughter, and I never tried to kid anybody else after that.

A celebrity is a person who works hard all his life to become known, then wears dark glasses to avoid being recognised.

Fred Allen

Fame lost its appeal for me when I went into a public restroom and an autograph seeker handed me a pen and paper under the toilet door.

Marlo Thomas

Celebrity is never more admired than by the negligent.

William Shakespeare

It is a short walk from the hallelujah to the hoot.

Vladimir Nabokov

Now there is fame! Of all – hunger, misery, the incomprehension by the public – fame is by far the worst. It is the castigation of God by the artist. It is sad. It is true.

Pablo Picasso

Losing a true friend

I was extremely fond of my two beautiful English setters who spanned thirty years of my life. We used to walk for miles every day in the rolling Berkshire countryside. It didn't really matter what the weather was like because nothing stopped our walks. Indeed, the more inclement the weather, the more exciting our walks became. I felt indomitable and brave striding out through driving rain with Tallis's tail waving like a flag above the long grass. Yes, both my setters were called Tallis after the English composer.

When the first Tallis died I grieved for a long time. I felt I had lost a lifelong and devoted friend. This lovely poem was sent to me by a friend on hearing of my loss. I'm afraid the writer is unknown to me:

DOG O' MINE

Dear dog, I miss you so – and yet
'Tis selfish of me to regret
And wish to have you back again,
You who at last are freed from pain.
I wonder if your loving heart
Knew that the time had come to part:
I think you did, for in your eyes
Flickered, methought, a grieved surmise
That this, alas, must be the end,

The dread good-bye of man and friend.
I could have wished that death had crept
On you, unwitting, as you slept:
It would have helped me, pal so true,
To feel 'At least, he never knew.'
If . . . somehow . . . somewhere . . . it may be
That you are conscious still of me,
Remember this – you gave me more
Than ever friend gave friend before;
To you I owe . . . *('Nay, Master! Set
your love for me against the "debt"'!)*

Author unknown

The return

'I've got to get back!' These were the exact words I spoke when one day I found that I had finally and completely gone to pieces over the death of my dog.

What I meant was that I wanted to go back to all the security and confidence of my childhood. The bliss of walking through the fields, reading my book in the hayloft, the warmth of the sun shining through the skylight, sitting beside Granny as she told me stories. These images came to mind as I tried to distract myself from all the grown-up issues I now had to face. I wanted to escape back to my uncomplicated past.

Warm days of summer,
Wandering through dusty lanes,
Strange! I can only remember the warm days,
When I escape back to childhood. Winter snow crisp and even,
Bright starry nights of frosty magic,
Strange! I can only remember
The clear bright skies of winter,
When I escape back to childhood. The sound of your voices,
the laughter, the play,
The crimson of a summer dawn,
In the whizzing of a pleasant wind,
Whispering across the hills
I remember you all,
In my escape back to childhood.

Hazel McIntyre

Welcome back

I was simply devastated at the loss of my first setter. I grieved for him over a long period and became really very depressed. I went down into the depths. People were very kind, and Jack said he would get me another puppy, but I knew it wasn't just the dog that was causing my depression. There was much more to it than that.

When I had been out walking with my dog, God had been reminding me of a peace that I could not find elsewhere. There were shades of feeling as close to my Maker as I had felt as a child, and now those walks had stopped.

One day I was sitting in the orchard by my home looking at the little mound where he was buried, and it suddenly became very clear to me. When I had been out walking the dog, I had been surrounded by the beauty of God's creation. It made me feel so content. I had, without being aware of it, been worshipping in the same way that I had done on the farm as a child. God had used the death of my beloved dog to draw me back to himself.

I went down to our local church, and sat at the back wondering what to do next. I knelt down and said, 'Father God, I'm really sorry that I left you.' I asked God to forgive me, and I knew from having read the Scriptures as a child that he would. I stood up a different person that day, and from that moment on, my life was to change in a way that fame and fortune couldn't change it. I have continued to ask God for his forgiveness on a daily basis. I'm human and I make many mistakes, but I know that his immense love is always the antidote.

CONSCIENCE

If I could shut the gate against my thoughts
And keep out sorry from this room within,
Or memory could cancel all the notes
Of my misdeeds, and I unthink my sin:
How free, how clear, how clean my soul should lie
Discharged of such a loathsome company!

Or were there other rooms within my heart
That did not to my conscience join so near,
Where I might lodge the thoughts of sin apart
That I might not their clamorous crying hear;
What peace, what joy, what ease should I possess,
Freed from their horrors that my soul oppress!

But, O my Saviour, who my refuge art,
Let thy dear mercies stand twixt them and me
And be the wall to separate my heart
So that I may at length repose me free;
That peace, and joy, and rest may be within,
And I remain divided from my sin.

Author unknown

Divine appointment

After I renewed my faith in God in the village church I met a charming woman, appropriately named Lydia, while out shopping. She persuaded me to visit her house each Wednesday morning where a group met for prayers and Bible study. I received good teaching there and was plied with books and Christian tapes that fed my appetite for knowledge of God after many years of being estranged from him. It seemed as though God had pre-arranged our meeting because at that time what I needed most was encouragement and teaching, and there was Lydia in the butcher's shop offering me just that.

I had never met her before and she had no idea when she spoke to me that I was someone who needed her help. It was wonderful proof to me that God was watching and guiding me.

Lydia and her friends assured me that God loved me enough to search me out, and would take delight in my return.

> Lord, you seized me and I could not resist you
> I ran for a long time, but you followed me.
> I took by-paths, but you knew them.
> You overtook me.
> I struggled,
> You won.
> Here I am, Lord, out of breath, no fight left in me, and
>   I've said 'yes' almost unwillingly.
> When I stood there trembling like one defeated before
>   his captor,
> Your look of love fell on me.

The die is cast, Lord, I can no longer forget you.
In a moment you seized me,
In a moment you conquered me.
My doubts were swept away,
My fears dispelled.
For I recognized you without seeing you.
I felt you without touching you.
I understood you without hearing you.

Marked by the fire of your love, I can no longer forget
   you.
Now I know that you are there, close to me, and I work
   in peace beneath your loving gaze.
I no longer know what it is to make an effort to pray.
I just lift my eyes to you and I meet yours.
And we understand each other. All is light, all is peace.

At times, O Lord, you steal over me irresistibly, as the
   ocean slowly covers the shore,
Or suddenly you seize me as the lover claps his beloved in
   his arms.
And I am helpless, a prisoner, and I have to stand still.
Captivated, I hold my breath, the world fades away, you
   suspend time.
I wish that these minutes were hours . . .
When you withdraw, leaving me as fire and overwhelmed
   with profound joy,
Though I have no new ideas, I *know* that you possess me
   more completely.
You have reached new depths in me,
The wound has widened and I am more than ever a
   prisoner of your love.
Lord, once more you have made a desert around me, but
   this time it is different.

You are too great, you eclipse everything.
What I had cherished now seems trifling, and my desires
    melt
Like wax in the sun under the fire of your love.
Nothing matters to me,
Neither my comfort
Nor even my life.
I desire only you,
I want nothing but you.

I know that the others say, 'He is mad!'
But, Lord, it is they who are out of their minds.
They do not know you, they do not know God, they do
    not know that one cannot resist him.
But you have seized me, Lord, and I am sure of you.
You are there, and I am overjoyed.
Sunlight floods over all, and my life shines like a jewel.
How easy everything is, how luminous!
All is pure and joyful.

Thank you, Lord, thank you!
Why me, why did you choose me?
Joy, joy, tears of joy.

Michel Quoist

God delights in me!

Imagine, God would take delight in me – yes, me – with my flat feet and lack of direction. He would wrap me in his love and quieten my fears. He would be happy and sing with joy, and best of all he would save me – save me from myself through his grace, so mysterious and desirable. What proof had I that he would do all this? His word is proof enough for me. I knew that God does not make rash promises, and therefore I knew I could trust him.

When you discover that you are loved by someone, it's a terrific boost to your confidence. Knowing you are loved by God is the greatest confidence boost of all. And yet still sometimes while praying I've suddenly caught my breath with the thought 'Is God really there? Does he really listen to me, or am I just deluding myself?'

My friends have assured me that everyone has doubting moments, and that I must remind myself of those times when God has been very real to me, and hang on to them. These memories help to cancel the doubts and I can pray with confidence:

Father God, thank you for loving us, and through your love strengthening us, so that we can go forward in the full assurance of knowing that we are your children, and that nothing can ever separate us from your love. Amen.

Spiritual workout

As an actor I find I am unable to give my best if I have not spent much time studying my script and thinking about the character I am about to play. This is true even with something light-hearted such as a pantomime. Like an athlete who wins the race by training, so my efforts to consider my role provide greater insight, meaning and actually make the whole process easier.

So it is with God. I find that when I spend less time with him, I can be reduced to 'weather talk' very quickly. When I chat to him each day, the relationship is so much easier to maintain. This spiritual workout is quite simple and takes so little time, and yet can be so refreshing. It can recharge your spiritual batteries very quickly.

Here is a poem by Monique Nicole Fox that reminds me that our heavenly Father is the one who wants to carry our burdens. But will we let him?

Come to God
    all that are weary
    and burdened with life's weights
    let God lift you from dire straits

Come to God
    all that are overwhelmed
    and stressed
    let God lift you from the entire mess

Come to God
  all that are in need of guidance
  and help
  let God lift you out of that circumstance

Come to God
  all that are confused
  and in turmoil
  let God lift you out of the muddy waters, filth and quick
  sands soil

Come to God
  all that are run down
  and tired
  let God save you before you drown
  You will find Him the best weight lifter in town

Monique Nicole Fox

Such confidence

From a very early age I always had an absolute certainty that I was going to be an actor. Apart from an aunt who was an amateur thespian, there was no history in the family of any theatrical intent.

In the 1940s there remained within our community a feeling that actors were still rogues and vagabonds and that it was a particularly unsuitable profession for girls. I remember my mother advising me, 'Never tell your granny that you want to be an actress. Tell her you want to be a teacher.' If my parents had tried to stop me at the time, I would have run away because I was so determined to act. I didn't analyse it because the whole concept was simply part of my psyche. That was the way I was made and I just accepted it as such. Various knocks along the way, however, were to make me a little more sceptical about being over-confident.

It's a strange thing, but whenever as an actor you feel too puffed up with your own importance, something happens to bring you down a peg. Sometimes I think to myself, 'Gosh, I delivered that speech well,' and I'll immediately stumble over the next line. When I think I've excelled myself in a scene, the director will inform me that it wasn't as good as the opening night.

I once played Maria in *Twelfth Night*. I was really enjoying myself portraying this feisty lady's maid and was looking forward to making my next entrance carrying a tray of goblets and a jug of ale. Feeling sure the audience couldn't wait to see me, I rushed on and fell flat on my face!

On another occasion, as the fairy in *Cinderella*, I made a

proud entrance in my glittering gown. The pyrotechnic flash announced my arrival, but unfortunately it went off under my crinoline and set fire to my dress. As I progressed downstage, trilling away, smoke was billowing from beneath my skirt. My legs began to get very hot and the conductor was hissing 'Get off the stage, Wendy, you're on fire!' I made my exit as gracefully as I could under the circumstances.

'You mustn't get above yourself, Wendy.' My mother's childhood admonishment still rings in my ears to this day.

Pride goes before destruction, a haughty spirit before a fall.

Proverbs 16:18, NIV

And God created rest

We are so confined by time. I must be getting older, for I just relish those days when nothing is in my diary. I feel wonderfully liberated when I don't have anything planned for a day. I actually think God made us to enjoy life, and not to work ourselves to death. God lives outside of time altogether: 'But, beloved, be not ignorant of this one thing, that one day is with the Lord as a thousand years, and a thousand years as one day' (2 Peter 3:8, AV).

According to Genesis, even though God worked hard creating the world, he rested on the seventh day, and built that rhythm into our world. If God needed to rest, then how much more do we! I do think it's sad that in our day and age we have eroded any form of 'Sabbath'. Even for those who are not churchgoers, every day of the week has become the same now. It means that we don't have a day that is put aside as different, a day to put up our feet, potter around, and regain our strength. Life is too demanding, and I'm sure that God never intended it to be that way. Rest is not an optional extra; it is vital in maintaining our physical, emotional and spiritual lives.

> Thank you, Lord,
> For this still pool of time,
> Its surface so unruffled.
> Calm sweet repose
> And rest in you.

These still waters
Of this quiet time
Reflect your face to me.
I sit and gaze.
I listen and I see now
With ears and eyes of faith.

No wind tosses these smooth waters
Of my pool.
It is a mirror
Shining back to me
The things of heaven.
It is encompassed by a stillness
Fit for you to come,
A place where eternity meets my 'now'.

F. M. Sarjeant

My Lord and my God, listening is hard for me. I do mean
exactly 'hard' for I understand that this is a matter of
receiving rather than trying. What I mean is that I am so
action orientated, so product driven, that doing is easier
for me than being. I need your help if I am to be still and
listen. I would like to try. I would like to learn how to sink
down into the light of your presence until I can become
comfortable in that posture.

Help me to try now. Amen.

Gerhard Tersteegen

Whenever I feel afraid

I did my first pantomime when I was fifty-nine. Quite late to start singing and dancing as a fairy, you might well say! I was really alarmed after I accepted the offer because I was quite ignorant of the genre and not sure I was up to it. I had an excellent teacher, though, in Jack Douglas, the comedian. He was directing the pantomime and also playing Baron Hardup. He is a charming man, fully experienced in every aspect of pantomime, and he gave me the confidence I needed.

The one thing he couldn't persuade me to do, though, was to sing 'live'. Since being discouraged from singing too loudly at school, I had always been very reluctant to open my mouth in song on stage. I therefore recorded my songs and mimed to them for the first eight performances, but Jack Douglas was not satisfied. He was determined to give me the confidence to stand up on stage and sing.

One day just before the matinee he came to me and said, 'Are you a professional artiste or not?' I could feel myself cringing because I knew what was coming.

'Well, yes, Jack, I like to think I am,' I replied shakily.

'In that case, how can you cheat the audience by miming your songs?' I knew he was right. Quaking, I agreed to sing live at the matinee.

As the moment approached I could feel my mouth go dry and my heart thump. The conductor gave me my intro, I took a deep breath, opened my mouth and sang, and away I went, throwing myself into it for all I was worth.

I discovered that I loved singing and always insisted on a

couple of songs in all the pantos I did after that. Thank you, Jack
Douglas, for letting your integrity brush off on me.

> Whenever I feel afraid
> I hold my head erect
> And whistle a happy tune
> So no-one will suspect I'm afraid
>
> While shivering in my shoes
> I strike a careless pose
> And whistle a happy tune
> And no-one ever knows I'm afraid
>
> The result of this deception is very strange to tell
> For when I fool the people I fear
> I fool myself as well!
>
> I whistle a happy tune
> And every single time
> The happiness in the tune
> Convinces me that I'm not afraid
>
> Make believe you're brave
> And the trick will take you far
> You may be as brave as you make believe you are.
> You may be as brave as you make believe you are.

Oscar Hammerstein II

Waiting in the wings

That moment when I am waiting in the wings for my first entrance is always the worst, even after all these years of performing. I stand there feeling very shaky and dry-mouthed, my heart beats very fast, and I'm still nervous, even after doing the same play for weeks on end.

Some of this is due to my understanding that the audience (or most of them) have paid for their seats and deserve a professional performance, and I don't want to let them, myself or my colleagues down. I always stand there asking God to equip me mentally and physically to do the work that he chose me to do. I recommend anyone to ask God for his help in this way, because in my experience he will give it.

When you next find yourself 'standing in the wings' waiting for some news, or preparing for work, perhaps one of the following quotations will help. These are some of my favourite 'fear nots' from the Authorised Version:

> Genesis 26:24: . . . fear not, for I am with thee, and will bless thee . . .
>
> Exodus 14:13: Fear ye not, stand still, and see the salvation of the Lord . . .
>
> Deuteronomy 20:3–4: . . . let not your hearts faint, fear not, and do not tremble, neither be ye terrified . . . For the Lord your God is he that goeth with you, to fight for you against your enemies, to save you.
>
> Deuteronomy 31:6, 8: Be strong and of a good courage, fear not, nor be afraid of them: for the Lord thy

God . . . he it is that doth go before thee; he will be with thee, he will not fail thee, neither forsake thee . . .

Joshua 1:9: Have not I commanded thee? Be strong and of a good courage; be not afraid, neither be thou dismayed: for the Lord thy God is with you whithersoever thou goest.

Joshua 8:1: And the Lord said . . . Fear not . . .

Joshua 10:8: And the Lord said . . . Fear them not: for I have delivered them [your enemies] into thine hand . . .

Joshua 10:25: Fear not, nor be dismayed, be strong and of good courage: for thus shall the Lord do to all your enemies whom ye fight.

Judges 6:23: And the Lord said . . . Peace be unto thee; fear not, thou shalt not die.

2 Kings 6:16: Fear not: for they that be with us are more than they that be with them.

1 Chronicles 28:20: Be strong and of good courage, fear not . . . for the Lord God, even my God, will be with thee; he will not fail thee, nor forsake thee, until thou has finished all the work for the service of the house of the Lord.

2 Chronicles 10:15, 17: Be not afraid nor dismayed because of this great multitude, for the battle is not yours, but God's . . . You shall not need to fight this battle . . . stand still and see the salvation of the Lord with you . . . fear not, nor be dismayed, for the Lord your God is with you.

Saying goodbye too soon

It was in 1994 that I lost my husband. I miss him now, and I know I'll always miss him. Fortunately, just before he died, Jack made a commitment to Christ so I know that he is safe in heaven. This brings me enormous comfort. I'll meet him again.

The time that he spent with me will always be cherished. When I needed reassurance he would take hold of my hands and say, 'Here, take some of my strength.'

In every circumstance without him, I know what he would expect me to do and can often hear his voice encouraging me forward, 'Come on, Wend! Get on with it! Don't sit there moping.' He wouldn't have let me give up work or become reclusive. He loved life and wanted me to do the same.

There was a twenty-two-year age difference between us, and I met him when he was Jack Bentley, an important musician in his own right. As I mentioned earlier, almost the minute I saw him it was love at first sight. I wanted him long before he wanted me. I was twenty. I have found that a marriage can last across such a generation gap.

We had difficulties in our marriage, but I really loved him and had that marvellous security of knowing that he really loved me. That is what tided us through everything.

Jack was a wise man as well as being generous, and forgiving. During the spring of 1994 when his illness was going through its fatal progression I was asked to do pantomime at the De Montfort Hall in Leicester in December of that year. I was afraid to accept because I didn't want to leave Jack, but he was adamant that I should say yes. He told me it would be an excellent thing for me to be occupied and mixing with young people in the fun and hurly-burly that is panto. At that moment

I knew he was telling me he wouldn't be there at Christmas and that I would need the company and support of colleagues and the jolly atmosphere of the theatre.

He died on 22 April 1994, and of course his wise words came true. I survived that first lonely Christmas in a haze of coloured lights, sparkling backcloths, dancing teenagers, and hilarious comics. Laughing one minute and crying the next. I felt Jack's strong hand guiding me.

Life is a series of events happy and sad . . .
love, marriage, the birth of a child;
the loss of one deeply loved, hurt relationships.

In time we understand more of life's meaning,
recognizing each event as a chance to reinforce our love
and confirm the value and joy of living.

With each new opportunity to grow,
challenges pull us closer to facing our mortality and
enrich our appreciation of the gifts that we have been given.

In facing an event that defies resolution,
we need a friend – a partner.
My silent partner . . .
my faith in God's understanding and love –
is an endless reservoir of strength.

We make our lives what they are.
My deep faith in God and my church
channels my strengths to overcome difficult obstacles
and appreciate life's pleasant surprises alike.

God's gift of faith is the guiding hand
that makes me the person that I need to be –
closer to His image,
continuing to grow and accept His love.

Frank Labaty

Sleeping in peace

I admit it. I don't sleep well. Often I wake in the night, my heart beating fast with anxiety and unknown dread. It may be one of the failings of growing older, the inability to sleep right through the night – that, and the need to go to the loo!

I make it a habit before I fall asleep to go through the day marking in my mind all the good things that have happened, and saying thank you to God for his gifts that day. Obviously this is a far better way of achieving a restful night than mulling over all the bad things, but it's not infallible.

If I find my mind is so alert that I know it's going to be impossible to sleep again for hours, I make a hot drink and read for a while, or else I pray about whatever it is that's making me anxious until I feel calmer. It's much better than lying there staring into the dark, I find, and usually I drop off again for an hour or two.

COURAGE FOR THE NIGHT

Lord of the evening
The day has passed
But the day's problems are still with me.
Sometimes I wish the day away,
I long for the night,
Hoping that sleep
Will envelop my difficulties,

Banish them forever
Beneath the blanket of darkness;
That I might rise to a fresh, new day
With my slate wiped clean.
But day follows day
And I am the same person
With the same problems, questions, difficulties.

Lord, I wish I could stand at a distance,
Far away from today,
Then perhaps I could smile
At today's problems.
If I look at last year's worries
Or even last month's
I know for a fact that I survived,
And that gives me hope.
But I don't want to run away
Or live my life at a distance,
I want to enjoy
The daily battle of life
As I live it.

Lord, fill my dreams tonight
With your spirit
So that I may face the world
Armed with these gifts
That nothing can destroy.

Frank Topping

Lady Kitty

After the death of my second English setter, I found the house very empty. There is no question about it, the presence of an animal in the house is comforting and companionable and I felt the quiet emptiness when I returned from work after the chatter and laughter on the set.

I came back two years ago after a theatre tour and thought how lovely it would be to have a pet to stroke and talk to. My thoughts must have been heard. The following day there was a loud miaow outside my back door. I looked through the glass pane, and there, sitting in the yard, was a rather dishevelled tabby cat. I was tempted to invite her in, but I was held back by the thought that I shouldn't encourage her because I am working away from home a great deal, and anyway she might belong to someone. Thinking about it, I had glimpsed her in the bushes a few times. She must have been eyeing my house as a possible home.

She stayed in the yard for a while and intermittently gave her very pathetic mew. One day I went shopping, and when I returned she jumped on to the car bonnet, staring at me with huge appealing eyes. My heart melted. I cut up a cold sausage and gave it to her, and from that moment on she decided to stay. Once she had acquired entry into the house, she claimed it as her own.

I tried every way to discover who owned her and where she had come from, but to no avail. I took her to the vet to see if she was micro-chipped. She wasn't, so I decided to have a chip put in, and gave my name as her owner. I put a cat flap in the door and named her Lady Kitty after the part I had just been playing, and because she was very much a lady cat.

She had wormed her way into my heart. She is a very self-contained little creature, a great hunter of small mammals and very sparing with her affection, but I love and admire her.

I have to arrange an army of people to feed her and to talk to her when I am away, but when I return she welcomes me with loud purring, twining her warm little body around my ankles. For my lifestyle she is quite perfect, and I am convinced she is a very special gift from God.

My garden is still an inspirational place for me. Although I no longer dig, I weed and plant as the mood takes me, often after a hard day in the studio; or, on a rare day off, I spend as much time as possible just being in it. Sitting in it, walking round it, pottering about, brings me such a sense of peace and tranquillity. It's also a great place to do my voice exercises without disturbing anybody!

One of my favourite places is my greenhouse. It's not a smart wooden one, just one of those quickly assembled structures, but it has over the years produced amazing crops of tomatoes, peppers, aubergines and melons. It has lovely open views across to Cliveden and it is a quiet warm place to sit and think. I don't grow things in it any longer because I'm away from home quite a lot and I can't keep it watered, but Lady Kitty has a spare bed in there and she's taken possession of it as a second home.

The cat is domestic only as far as it suits its own ends; it will not be kennelled or harnessed nor suffer any dictations as to its goings out or comings in. Long contact with the human race has developed in it the art of diplomacy, and no Roman Cardinal of medieval days knew better how to ingratiate himself with his surroundings than a cat with a saucer of cream on its mental horizon.

Saki

Come lovely cat, and
Rest upon my heart,
And let my gaze dive in
The cold
Live pools of thine enchanted
Eyes that dart
Metallic rays of green
And gold.

Charles Pierre Baudelaire

PANDORA

Dear sweet cat with your surprised eyes and sunlit fur, what joy
to lie beneath the tree, with you singing in my hair.

Carla Lane

Unwrapping the gifts

I'm quite sure my little cat was a gift. These lines about opening gifts were sent to me recently. There's an ocean of truth in them:

Babies can't open their gifts. Mum or Dad does it for them.

A young child/teenager opens their gifts fast and is only looking for what they wanted. When they get the package opened, they quickly go on to the next one. When they are done, they are 'bored' already.

An adult opens their package slowly – they enjoy every bit of it. Some will even study how well it was wrapped (much to the impatience of the kids) and will keep the wrapping paper. When the gift is open, they are very thankful and take some time to enjoy it right away.

An older person is just happy the whole family are there – they have had plenty of gifts and understand and appreciate them all. They enjoy watching the family members open their gifts.

We open our gifts from God in the same way:

A baby Christian can't open any of their gifts. They have no idea how to. Their 'mum/dad' must do it for them. Their friends – their pastor – open the Book and show the baby Christian all the gifts that God has given them, but unfortunately, just like a baby, they don't really understand yet the greatness of those gifts.

A child/teen Christian is anxious to get what *they* want from God. They hear about the gifts, but if the gifts are not of interest to them, they just push them aside for now. Eventually, many of them become bored with their Christian life and want more of what they want, not what God has given them.

An 'adult' Christian enjoys all the gifts from God. They take their Book and, as they open each gift, they study it carefully and fully appreciate the entire gift and what it means to them.

An older Christian is just happy to see the family members getting their gifts and enjoy watching them as they learn about what God has done for them – you see, they have all been there before in their earlier years.

I'm sure God watches all this with great patience!

A new day, every day!

My bedroom window faces the sunset and my kitchen window catches the sunrise. I am tempted to stand and watch these happenings as often as possible, mesmerised by the excitement and beauty of it all.

God is the most amazing Creator and he is still creating. There's a new sunrise and sunset every single day. How wonderful a daily gift!

> I have seen the sun break through
> To illuminate a small field
> For a while, and gone my way
> And forgotten it. But that was the pearl
> Of great price. The one field that had
> Treasure in it. I realise now
> That I must give all that I have
> to possess it. Life is not hurrying
> on to a receding future, nor hankering after
> an imagined past. It is the turning
> aside like Moses to the miracle
> of the lit bush, to a brightness
> that seemed as transitory as your youth
> once, but is the eternity that awaits you.

R. S. Thomas

My mother's homecoming

My mother suffered from dementia. It was tragic to watch her slow decline. She was aware that something was happening to her mind, but she was proud and brave, and she pretended she hadn't noticed. She kept herself looking smart, choosing each morning what clothes to wear, and applying powder, lipstick and blusher like a young girl. Her hair had been black, thick and lustrous and she had been proud of it. She asked me to put it in rollers and then to brush and style it for her.

Gradually she became confused, forgetful, and lost all sense of time, putting on her clothes and waiting to be taken to the shops in the middle of the night. For her own safety, we had to find her a residential home. It was heartbreaking, but my husband was dying of cancer and I couldn't take care of them both. It was the saddest thing I ever had to do, but she never let me see her pain. She loved me too much. A dear lady carer, called Peggy, helped to make her new life comfortable and cheerful, and my brother, his wife Dorothy, and friends rallied round with visits and outings. She died a year after Jack. I think of her and miss her every single day, but I am comforted in the knowledge that while I was sitting with her during the last days of her illness she cried out, 'Help me, Lord. Help me, Father.' I am trusting that the Lord heard her cry out to him and took her home.

And then, whoever calls out to the Lord for help will be saved.

Acts 2:21

THE CUSHION RING

I wore your ring today
'A cushion ring' they said when I bought it,
When I proudly bought it.
Asking the buxom lady behind the counter
To show it me on her white dimpled hand.
'For my mother's birthday' I told her
'She'll like it' the lady said
flashing the cushion ring
under the counter lights.
How proud I was to give it to you,
How pleased you were to take it.
Filigree trellis circle
Set about with garnets red.
Fit for a Queen.
Fit for my mother's lovely work worn hands.
Hands that had cared for me, cooked for me, cleaned for me.
Hands that had washed my hair,
wiped my nose,
buttoned my shoes, rocked me to sleep.
Today, I folded your hands, still warm, across your silent
   breast,
And their beauty is imprinted on my soul.
I wear your ring and long for you.
I pray that you are peaceful, happy, calm.
Your hands resting in your lap at last.

Wendy Craig

Heavenly music

Music has always had a big role to play in my life. I love it and need it. Nothing can alter my mood as quickly, or give me more pleasure, than music, and I listen to it whenever I can.

Our house was always full of music. Jack had a vast library of LPs, ranging from opera to Jack Teagarden. My eldest son Alaster studied the oboe and is now principal oboist with the Symphonia Royal Ballet, and my younger son, Ross, played the piano and enjoys playing in an exclusive semi-pro band. My granddaughters are very musical too. Julia is a flautist, Charlotte learnt the saxophone, and Madeleine is studying violin at the Birmingham Conservatoire. Emma is learning the flute at school. I am blessed to have been surrounded with so much beautiful music.

While on tour with *The Circle* in 2003, I went to Kings College, Cambridge, one Sunday evening to hear the choir sing Evensong. It was magnificent. The human voice can be a beautiful instrument, and when it is used to praise God, it is simply heavenly.

One of my favourite writers of music for choirs is John Rutter. He has written and arranged some superb music for choral singing. One piece of his I particularly love is his setting of the Gaelic Blessing:

> Deep peace of the running wave to you
> Deep peace of the flowing air to you
> Deep peace of the quiet earth to you
> Deep peace of the shining stars to you
> Deep peace of the gentle night to you

Moon and stars pour their healing light on you
Deep peace of Christ the light of the world to you
Deep peace of Christ to you . . .

John Rutter

Learning the lines

Learning lines is fundamental to any stage actor, because you can't start acting until you have memorised the lines, and they have become second nature to you. Learning lines has always been something I have had to work hard at, but some plays are worse than others.

I was to play the infamous role of Mrs Malaprop in a new 2003 production of *The Rivals* for the Royal Shakespeare Company, but I hadn't done anything on the stage, except pantomime, for several years. The role was very demanding in so many ways, and I wasn't quite sure that I was up to it. I was worried about learning the lines with all those malapropisms to get my tongue round. With no husband Jack to support me by hearing me rehearse my lines, I wasn't even sure that my memory was still able to cope with such a complicated script.

I was playing the good fairy in pantomime at Rhyl when the script arrived. When I read it, I knew exactly how I wanted to play the part of Mrs Malaprop, and hoped that the director felt the same way. By this time I started to panic, and so I wrote to Marie Laclave, an American pen friend to whom I would occasionally open my heart. I told her how scared I was to be playing Mrs Malaprop. She wrote back straight away with the words 'Be bold, and mighty forces will come to your aid.'

This was a direct quote from Canadian novelist and clergyman Basil King. He lived from 1859 to 1928, and was reminding us that we only struggle through life on our own if we choose to. It was a good quote for me. If mighty forces are going to aid me, then how could I fail? It reminded me of Romans 8:31 where it says, 'If God is for us, who can be against us?'

Well, in the coming weeks mighty forces did aid me. A dear friend in my village, Reca McGibbon, offered to come and hear my lines, which must be one of the most tedious jobs in the world, and something that requires enormous patience from the listener. She was very strict and made me go over and over them until they were word-perfect and I could recite them in my sleep. The rehearsals were strenuous but exciting, and Lindsay Posner, the director, and I saw eye to eye on the interpretation. The opening night went almost without a hitch, and the reviews were good. So be bold as you prepare to cross your own hurdles, face your own fears, and expect that 'mighty forces will come to your aid'.

God is with us to be utilized. His Power, His Love, His Thought, His Presence must be at our disposal, like other great forces, such as sunshine and wind and rain. We can use them or not, as we please. We can use them in proportion to our ability.

Basil King

Privacy made public

Being in the public eye means that I am sometimes reminded of my past wrongs in a very public way. When my privacy is compromised in the media and press, I just keep praying. I know it sounds pious, but what else can I do? I am not perfect and I never have been. What distresses me most is when my family and friends are hurt, but throughout they've been tremendously loyal and understanding and I shall always be grateful to them for their unconditional love. I also gain comfort from a Saviour who not only forgives, but also forgets. Thank God!

THE DEPTH OF YOUR LOVE

If I choose to remember my past sins
And my unenlightened soul,
It is not out of any love for them
But because I want to love you, my God.
It is in order to know the depth of your love
That I recall the wickedness of my past
In that bitter memory
My hope is to feel your sweetness,
A sweetness in which there is no deception,
Only happiness and security;
So I seek to restore unity within me
In the wake of those inner wounds
Which tore me apart

When I gave myself up to vain things
And turned away from you,
The one true God.

St Augustine of Hippo

Counting the seconds

I have got an old school clock on my living room wall. It has a kind 'face' and a gentle 'voice' when it ticks away, reminding me whether it's time to leave the house for work or slip into my bed at the end of the day. The seconds tick away quite loudly, but the sound has become so familiar that I am hardly aware of it any more. It's always set ten minutes fast to move me into action and remind me not to be late for appointments.

The constant 'tick-tock, tick-tock' could be saying 'slow-down, slow-down'. Perhaps we have such busy lives that we concentrate on the minutes, the hours and the days, and we miss those small precious seconds of life. I would like to slow the clock down and stop time ebbing away so fast, and yes I am sure that my clock would like to slow me down too.

SLOW ME DOWN, LORD

Ease the pounding of my heart by the quieting of my
    mind.
Steady my hurried pace with a vision of the eternal reach
    of time.
Give me, amid the confusion of the day, the calmness of
    the everlasting hills.
Break the tension of my nerves and muscles with the
    soothing music of the singing streams that live in my
    memory.

Help me to know the magical, restoring power of sleep.
Teach me the art of taking minute vacations – slowing
down to look at a flower, to chat with a friend, to pat
a dog, to read a few lines from a good book.
Slow me down, Lord, and inspire me to sink my roots
deep into the soil of life's enduring values that I may
grow toward the stars of my greater destiny.

Author unknown

The royal blessing

I am so pleased to be working on another ITV series of *The Royal*. It is now in its fifth series and I am still getting to grips with the irascible matron who rules the 1960s hospital with a rod of iron, and a soft heart.

The people I work with are talented, warm-hearted friends. We have become a family and we care about one another. On filming days I wake up feeling thoroughly blessed. Jobs for actors are few and far between. It is so easy to look around and feel that everyone is doing better than you are, but look a little wider and it is easy to see that's not true:

If you woke up this morning with more health than illness, you are more blessed than the million who will not survive the week.

If you have never experienced the danger of battle, the loneliness of imprisonment, the agony of torture or the pains of starvation, you are ahead of 500 million people around the world.

If you can express your beliefs without fear of harassment, arrest, torture or death, you are more blessed than almost three billion people in the world.

If you have food in your refrigerator, clothes on your back, a roof over your head and a place to sleep, you are richer than 75% of this world.

If you have money in the bank, in your wallet, and spare change in a dish someplace, you are among the top 8% of the world's wealthy.

If your parents are still married and alive, you are very, very rare.

If you hold up your head with a smile on your face and are truly thankful, you are blessed because the majority can, but most do not.

If you can hold someone's hand, hug them or even touch them on the shoulder, you are blessed because you can offer God's healing touch.

If you own just one Bible, you are abundantly blessed. One-third of the world does not have access to even one.

If you can read this message, you are more blessed than over two billion people in the world that cannot read anything at all.

Author unknown

Real stars

I was due to catch a train early one morning on the way up to Scarborough for another set of dates filming *The Royal*. I yawned as I got out of bed in the darkness. Having dressed, I grabbed my ready-packed suitcase and, arriving downstairs, made for the front door. Something made me stop.

'Of course. I must draw the curtains in the sitting room before I leave,' I thought.

Like a scene from some dramatic film, I gripped the curtains and drew them aside in one swift opening movement. The scene that greeted me was overwhelming. For there, twinkling in the blackness, were the greatest array of stars I had ever seen. The sky was shimmering with the bright myriads, which, whether a large planet or a tiny speck, were all glittering just as brightly.

I suddenly felt aware of the great expanse of the universe. Looking up into the dark, I had to smile as it occurred to me that the public nickname given to people who are well known was inappropriate.

'Now these are *real* stars,' I muttered. 'Not like we show-offs here on earth.'

STARS

Tonight the sky is calm
With the still, cool light of stars,
And yet they are not silent.
On such a night

The heavens salute their creator with shouts of joy
Too exquisite for the human ear.
Tonight is a festival.
Virtuoso performers take their places
From dazzling patterns
Brilliant clusters
And they are perfect.

And I have known them
These stars
From the days of my childhood
To the days of my children.
Walking down country lanes
We have identified the Plough
Pointed to the Pole
And felt small beneath their majesty.
On such a night I have held the North Star
Beneath the mainmast shrouds of a tall ship
Steering for home.
Ageless mariners have looked
To that constant star
And are looking, tonight.

Tonight, each star and planet
Is the splash of a sounding
Measuring depth of the Almighty.
Tonight there is so much laughter in the sky
Because you have filled it with old friends
Holding lanterns
And singing songs of love across the heavens.
And once again I know
That your light is ever before me.

Frank Topping

Hope for the future

My ambitions for the future are simple: I just want to keep working. I do love my work. I love mixing with other actors and enjoy the whole ambience of television and theatre. Of course, I'm hoping for some suitable roles to play as I get older. The older actresses like Margaret Rutherford and Thora Hird, who kept going to the end, are professional role models for me.

I have hope for my children and grandchildren too. My family is the future and I pray each day for their well-being and safety. They are loving and good to me, as well as being hard-working and socially involved. I am indeed blessed with a family to be proud of, and now there is someone new in my life. Three years ago, Ross and his lovely wife Kate presented me with another granddaughter, Iris. She has brought such joy, and each time I see her I feel renewed by her youth and innocence.

A WIDOW TO HER GRANDCHILD

Sweet new life,
You are to me a light that glows
In my darkest hour;
Though fate has closed a door
Behind me, your smile has opened
Windows on a new world,
Yet to be explored.
I look into your eyes and see

144

Before me hope and love to come;
I wait, to watch you grow
From babyhood to childhood,
And to hold your hand in mine
So we together can explore
Your world of wonderment and joy.
I can now fill my lonely hours
With thoughts of you, and dreams
Of happy years ahead,
And pray that as you grow
You will regard me as a friend.

A loving gift

My orchard is a special place, green and peaceful, separated from the rest of the garden by a low red-brick wall. My dogs are buried there, and I often sit under a large Bramley apple tree when I want to have time alone to think.

My sons, Alaster and Ross, have done so many kind things for me. No mother could have two more thoughtful sons. One of the precious things that Ross did after the death of my dog was to design and lay a little red-brick path from the garden gate through the orchard to my secret seat under the apple tree. He seemed to understand my sorrow so well, and set about creating his comforting gift with tenderness and affection. This little path is magical to me. I have planted snowdrops and bluebells along its edge, and soft green moss has formed in the cracks. Now I love to walk with his little daughter Iris into the orchard, armed with carrier bags to gather windfalls and watch her joy as she laughs and plays under the trees.

The source of love is deep in us and we can help others realise a lot of happiness. One word, one action, one thought can reduce another person's suffering and bring that person joy.

Thich Nhat Hanh

God of the open air

My final choice encompasses all that I hold dear, God's precious and beautiful gifts which continue to inspire my life and work as I move forward into the unknown:

These are the things I prize
And hold of dearest worth:
Light of the sapphire skies,
Peace of the silent hills,
Shelter of forests, comfort of the grass,
Music of birds, murmur of little rills,
Shadows of cloud that swiftly pass,
And, after showers,
The smell of flowers
And of the good, brown earth –
And best of all, along the way, friendship and mirth.
So let me keep
These treasures of the humble heart
In true possession, owning them by love;
And when at last I can no longer move
Among them freely, but must part
From the green fields and waters clear,
Let me not creep
Into some darkened room and hide
From all that makes the world so bright and dear;
But throw the windows wide
To welcome in the light;
And while I clasp a well-beloved hand,
Let me once more have sight

Of the deep sky and the far-smiling land –
Then gently fall on sleep,
And breathe my body back to Nature's care,
My spirit out to thee, God of the open air.

Henry van Dyke